I0426564

Understanding Cellular Metabolism

Nutrition, health and beauty*

2nd Edition
Leonard Sonnenschein
© 1/15/2014

Everything you learned about metabolism in your first science class is wrong! Every generation has become astounded by the advances in science made within their generation. This book will review what is known about cellular metabolism and how it governs your health. You will be amazed how the absorption of nutrients affects your wellness, your beauty, and your longevity. You will also find out that most nutritional supplements, most cosmetics, and, indeed, most pharmaceuticals are not designed for optimal absorption; therefore you are not getting the necessary nutrition and other benefits that you expect and need for your best life. You will find out about BOOSTER™, which is based on an organic and natural process of the cell that can change your life, and how its technology can be included in your consumer choice of the nutritional, pharmaceutical, and cosmetic products you use. Come explore this fascinating discovery that can help you!

*Proceeds from the sale of this book go to support the World Aquarium and its Conservation for the Oceans Foundation

UNDERSTANDING CELLULAR METABOLISM

By Leonard Sonnenschein

TABLE OF CONTENTS

Acknowledgments_____page 3

Foreword_____page 4

Preface_____page 5

Chapter 1: Introduction_____page 7

Chapter 2: Traditional Cell Metabolism & Immunology____page 17

Chapter 3: New Mechanisms for Understanding Cell Metabolism____page 26

Chapter 4: New Ideas for Cell Nutrition_____page 29

Chapter 5: Updating Cell Immunology_____page 31

Chapter 6: Delivery of Active Ingredients_____page 34

Chapter 7: Food Chemistry_____page 37

Chapter 8: Setting New Absorption Standards_____page 43

Chapter 9: Adopting New Patterns for Cosmetics_____page 60

Chapter 10: Advances in Chemotherapy_____page 62

Chapter 11: Other Uses for Enhanced Delivery (spray analgesics, etc.)____page 65

Chapter 12: Toxin Absorption_____page 67

Chapter 13: Topical Botox®_____page 70

Chapter 14: New Frontiers_____page 72

Chapter 15: Agricultural Applications_____page 73

Chapter 16: GroFish™ Technology_____page 79

Chapter 17: Aquacultural Feed Applications_____page 89

Chapter 18: Conclusion and What You Can Do_____page 94

About the Author_____page 95

Bibliography by Chapter_____page 96

Index_____page 108

Acknowledgments

I would like to acknowledge the following people who helped make this book possible:

Kara Warren for untiringly providing editorial research support, compiling the manuscript, providing analysis of chemistry relationships to cellular metabolism, and remaining in good spirits in making sure the job got done.

Many thanks to Terra Fletcher for her beautiful drawings that convey a vast amount of information using imagination and style.

Robert Montgomery, senior writer of BASS Publications, for his initial review of the manuscript and recommendations.

The World Aquarium Staff in supporting the bench-level research through animal care and husbandry for research systems.

Dr. Bill Longmore for his eight years in helping supervise research interns.

Dr. Lon Wilkens for helping to design the initial research platform for the World Aquarium.

Dr. Charles R. Granger for being an inspiration for inquiry learning.

Over three hundred interns who have come to the World Aquarium since 1992 to engage in applied-science research projects that expanded knowledge of sustainable aquaculture, sustainable agriculture, coral reef ecology, eutrophic zone chemistry, and climate change adaptation.

Foreword

I welcome this opportunity to provide a foreword for *Understanding Cellular Metabolism*. In my thirty years of experience in the pharmaceutical and nutraceutical health markets, I have been involved with the promotion of various products to improve people's lives.

As a vice president at Rexall-Sundown, I was involved in distributing products to over one hundred thousand stores that served millions of people. As owners of the rights associated with glucosamine chondroitin, the largest distributed nutraceutical product that has given relief to arthritis and other joint pain sufferers, we became involved with marketing nutraceuticals to the largest retail sellers of products in the world. All of these products dealt with active and inactive ingredients, where delivery of these ingredients was important from the medical standpoint as well as from the business standpoint.

As I have read this book, I realize that all of these relationships and, indeed, services to the patient and consumer are based upon the cellular ability to absorb nutrients and other active ingredients, and understanding the cell's ability to absorb these nutrients and active ingredients depends upon the makeup of the products being used. I believe that the knowledge in this book will change the entire model for the nutraceutical, pharmaceutical, and cosmetic markets.

I welcome the heightening of the consumer's awareness of how better science can bring them better health and, from a business standpoint, look forward to consumers demanding better products that deliver active ingredients in better ways to allow them to better enjoy life.

Jim Airaghi

Nutritional Alliance Inc.

Preface

This book lays the foundation for the advanced reader to better understand cell metabolism and the processes for health and active ingredient uptake in cells. A second book will be published soon for the general public that can be used to inform the consumer about their choices for health and nutrition, especially regarding vitamins, minerals, and cosmetics applications.

Recently there have been several medical journal articles about the effectiveness of vitamins for treating patients for cancer and heart disease and for the use of supplements. These articles stated that there is no statistical benefit for high-dose administered multivitamins for the patient and indeed an editorial was written for the Annals of Internal Medicine stating that there was no generalized benefit for taking these multivitamins in high doses. Alternatively, this book will argue that the delivery system needs to be looked at in the application for high dose and regular applications for vitamin therapy and prophylactic use that had been traditionally indicated for general good health.

The author of this book commissioned an independent study to look at the effectiveness of high-dose administration of vitamin D3 compared to high-dose administration of vitamin D3 using the BOOSTER delivery system which yielded a 9.8x increase in vitamin D3 uptake compared to the high dose control. Therefore, the application and delivery of the vitamin - mineral complex is very important in how it relates to the recommended daily allowance in the determination at the cellular level what is actually available for metabolic utilization. In other words, if you take a pill and little to none of the active ingredients are absorbed, then it is logical to estimate that taking the pill will be ineffective to improving one's health.

This book delves deeply into the issues of delivery of nutrition and other products for health and beauty and gives practical ideas for the consumer to consider based on biochemistry principles.

How Does This Mechanism Work?

Imagine: when you eat, it is common to use salt to enhance the flavor of the food. The reaction of the salt in solution enhances the ability of your taste buds to recognize the active ingredients in the food, giving desirability to the food. It does this by opening up cell pores to allow intercellular absorption of those food ingredients, triggering gratification. Also in this process nerves are stimulated, and in response hormone stimulation is also achieved. Indeed it is this same type of recognition and transmission system that can work for other active health, nutrition, and cosmetic products. Of course, the amount of salt used is directly related to the intensity of the reaction and can be used in conjunction with other adjuvants, just as garlic salt or pepper can be added to salt for additional flavor enhancement.

Salt in higher quantities can also be used to stimulate an inflammatory response such as in the case of GroFish™ treatment, whereby the cells are stimulated into a reactive state that increases blood flow, modulates protein synthesis, and induces an immunologic cascade and subsequent intercellular organelle enhancement. Using very young animals in the GroFish™ treatment causes a majority of the whole animal's cells to reset at a heightened level for the overall metabolism of the animal including health surveillance aspects.

Also, by changing the composition of what is outside of the cell membrane, pores or channels can be opened to allow larger molecules to enter, thereby increasing the absorption of active ingredients. Also, by using salt as a stimulant, the cell wall can modulate cell organelles in number and activity to affect the physiology of the cell. With these heightened abilities for absorption and physiology, immunity is also increased.

Please enjoy this book as a trip through understanding how the cell works and ways that you can improve your diet, your use of cosmetics, and other nutraceutical products to improve your health and beauty.

The purpose of this book is to inform about ideas regarding cellular metabolism and how they might affect consumers' decisions in health, beauty and nutrition. The book is not intended as a sales tool or to replace the professional advice a person should seek to treat illness or to make other decisions regarding health, beauty or nutrition. The book references a number of resources that the consumer can further research. The book helps fulfill the mission of the World Aquarium as an educational tool for the public and conveys scientific mechanisms regarding conservation that as adopted can improve our relationships with nature. Thank you for your support! I have left blank spaces throughout the book purposely with the hope that you make notes and personalize your experience in your exploration toward better nutrition, health and beauty.

I wish you good reading!

Sincerely yours in conservation and education with your good health in mind,

Leonard Sonnenschein
President
World Aquarium and Conservation for the Oceans Foundation
www.worldaquarium.org
www.cfto.org

Chapter 1. Introduction

In this chapter, we will discover what cells are and how they work.

- Overview of ideas and why we should study this;
- Analysis of the whole by breaking it into the smallest operating parts;
- Study of the history of the cell and its functional components and organelles; and
- Examination of defining standards.

According to the World Health Organization, the global pharmaceuticals market is worth US$300 billion a year, a figure expected to rise to US$400 billion within three years (World Health Organization, 2013). The global nutrition market is forecasted to exceed $400 billion by 2014 (Transparency Market Research Blog, 2013). World health care expenditures are estimated to be over US$9 trillion per year. The aim of pharmaceutical and nutritional companies is to create enhanced delivery to, or uptake by target cells, of active ingredients. Our research shows a primary flaw in the current understanding of the model of delivery of active ingredients.

A recent study (Global Sherpa, 2013) showed the capacity of the longevity of cells to be influenced by nutritional status. Nutrition to cells occurs with protein, minerals, and vitamin availability (Casiday and Frey, 2013). Other environmental factors also influence the uptake of these metabolic products (Bennett, 2013). The cells themselves over time may also show loss of intercellular competence over time due to genetic losses due to stressors on the mitotic and meiotic processes.

Our current research has identified a new mechanism for understanding cell metabolism, which is controlled by the cell membrane (Sonnenschein, 2013). BOOSTER™, a patent-pending process utilizing this mechanism, enhances the uptake of active ingredients in pharmaceutical, nutraceutical, and cosmetic markets.

Recent patent-pending understanding of how to improve the delivery of active ingredients (Sonnenschein, Leonard, Methods and compositions for enhancing the uptake of an active ingredient, US Provisional Application #61/716331, filed October 17, 2012) is expected to have profound effects on the medical, pharmaceutical, nutritional, cosmetic, and homeopathic industries. This metabolic process has opened up a new territory of cellular metabolism by identifying the cell membrane as the controller rather than the nucleus ("New Mechanisms to Understanding the Cell Membrane's Role in Modulating Intercellular Metabolism for Nutritional Delivery," Swedish University of Agricultural Sciences). The capacity of the cell membrane for transfer of essential nutrition can be enhanced even to the novel delivery of large molecules that may further benefit cellular metabolism as demonstrated by Leonard Sonnenschein in his patent from 2001 (Sonnenschein, Leonard, Method of stimulating growth in aquatic animals, US Patent 6,238,706, issued May 29, 2001), which shows the ability to move large protein synthesis stimulator molecules into the cell.

Additionally, as the cell membrane has a front-line role in protein recognition that renders immunologic capacity, the new methodology has shown the ability to improve immunosurveillance of the cell to bacterial and viral theta, yielding healthier individuals when exposed to pathogens (Luecke and Sonnenschein, 2013). By being able to modulate the cellular uptake of nutrients and influence the competency of the cell wall, anti-aging effects are logical next steps for human, animal, and even plant biology.

Independent laboratory analysis (GVK, Hyderabad, India) of the efficacy of BOOSTER™ has been conducted. Male mice were administered vitamin D_3 along with a control or a BOOSTER™-supplemented diet. The objective of this study was to determine the urine concentrations of vitamin D_3 in mice after oral administration of vitamin D_3 incorporated in the diet at 25,000 IU. The BOOSTER™-treated urine concentration of vitamin D_3 was 9.8 times higher than the control group. Therefore, BOOSTER™ very significantly increased the absorption of vitamin D_3 in this mammalian model.

This newly identified active-ingredient delivery system will allow for using less raw product in formulations with a more efficient delivery, a significantly decreased price, increased potency, and potentially reduced side effects, thereby creating a new model for improving the human health condition.

HISTORY
The starting point for the study of cells might be considered the 1830s. Though scientists had been using microscopes for centuries, they were not always sure what they were looking at. Robert Hooke's initial observation in 1665 of plant-cell walls in slices of cork was followed shortly by Antonie van Leeuwenhoek's first descriptions of live cells with visibly moving parts (Miko, 2013). In the 1830s two scientists who were colleagues—Schleiden, looking at plant cells, and Schwann, looking first at animal cells—provided the first clearly stated definition of the cell

(Miko, 2013). Their definition stated that that all living creatures, both simple and complex, are made out of one or more cells, and the cell is the structural and functional unit of life (Miko, 2013).

The purpose of a cell is to carry out a specific function through interactions with its environment for the purposes of maintaining the organism. These functions include growing, reproducing, responding to changes in the environment, moving, and metabolizing food for fuel.

How an Animal Cell Works
All animals are made up of tiny cells. Each one of these cells can grow, reproduce, respond to changes in the environment, move, and metabolize food for fuel. Tiny structures inside the cell called organelles work together to carry out all the cell's life functions. Although technology has enabled our knowledge to advance, much has remained unchanged about how a cell works.

Three Basic Parts of the Cell
An animal cell is made up of three basic parts: the cell membrane, the nucleus, and the protoplasm. The cell membrane is considered to be the gatekeeper of the cell, following the commands of the nucleus. The cell membrane keeps the cell together, separates each cell from other cells, and allows the transport of ions in and out of the cell. It is widely assumed that the nucleus controls this transport, but our research shows differently.

The nucleus is the cell's control center and directs growth, metabolism, and reproduction. It contains the chromosomes that contain the genetic instructions for making all the cell's proteins.

The material inside the cell is called protoplasm consisting of mostly water, salts (like sodium, potassium, calcium, and magnesium), proteins, lipids, and carbohydrates and is the major part of the cell. The protoplasm has two parts: the nucleoplasm (inside the nucleus) and the cytoplasm (outside of the nucleus). The fluid part of cytoplasm is called the cytosol. Floating within the cytosol are organelles, tiny metabolic components that perform a specific job to maintain the life of the cell.

Cross-Section of an Animal Cell

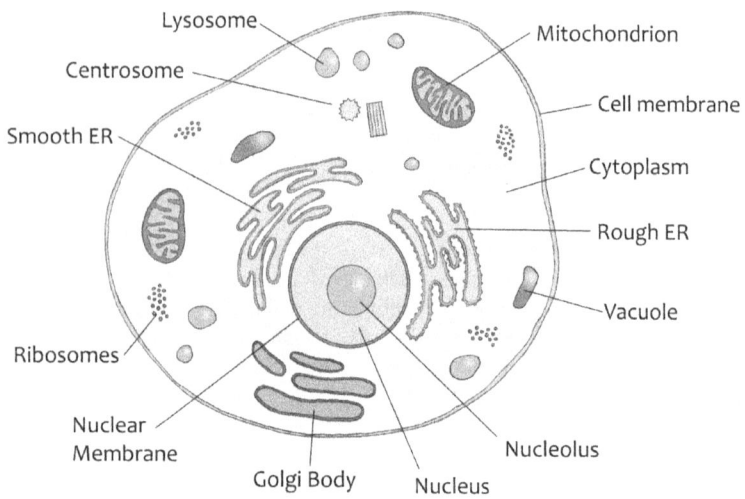

Here is a list of the parts of a cell and their definitions:

Cell membrane - the thin layer of protein and fat that surrounds the cell. The cell membrane is semipermeable, allowing some materials to pass into the cell and blocking others.

Cytoplasm - the substance between the cell membrane and the nucleus in which the organelles are located containing a liquid called cytosol.

Golgi body (also called the Golgi apparatus and/or Golgi complex) - an organelle, consisting of layers of flattened sacs, that acts as a machine in-taking and processing products from the endoplasmic reticulum and then releasing the finished products into the cell cytoplasm or secreting them outside of the cell.

Lysosome - round organelles surrounded by a membrane and containing digestive enzymes, the site of where digestion of cell nutrients takes place.

Mitochondrion – 'hot dog' shaped organelles with a double membrane that are the energy mechanisms of the cell, turning stored glucose into ATP (adenosine triphosphate) for the cell.

Nuclear membrane - a membrane that surrounds the nucleus.

Nucleolus - an organelle located within the nucleus that produces ribosomal RNA.

Nucleus - spherical body containing many organelles, including the nucleolus. The nucleus controls many of the functions of the cell including protein synthesis (chromosomal and DNA driven). The nucleus is surrounded by the nuclear membrane.

Ribosome - small organelles composed of RNA-rich cytoplasmic granules that are sites of protein synthesis.

Rough endoplasmic reticulum (rough ER) - a vast system of interconnected, membranous, enfolded, and convoluted sacs that are located in the cell's cytoplasm. Rough ER is covered with ribosomes that give it a rough appearance. Rough ER transports materials through the cell and produces proteins in sacs called cisternae (which are sent to the Golgi body, or inserted into the cell membrane).

Smooth endoplasmic reticulum (smooth ER) - a vast system of interconnected, membranous, enfolded and convoluted tubes that are located in the cell's cytoplasm (the ER is continuous with the outer nuclear membrane). The space within the ER is called the ER lumen. Smooth ER transports materials through the cell. It contains enzymes and produces and digests lipids (fats) and membrane proteins; smooth ER buds off from rough ER, moving the newly made proteins and lipids to the Golgi body, lysosomes, and membranes.

Vacuole - fluid-filled, membrane-surrounded cavities inside a cell. The vacuole fills with food being digested and waste material that is on its way out of the cell.

CELL COMPONENT COMPARISON:		
	Animal Cell versus	**Plant Cell**
Shape	round	rectangular
Centrioles	present in all	only present in lower plant forms
Vacuole	one or more –small	one large – up to 90% of cell volume
Chloroplasts	none	present in all plants, convert light to food
Lysosomes	present	rarely
Plastids	none	present

Both animal and plant cells have cell membranes, cytoplasm, endoplasmic reticulum, ribosomes, mitochondria, Golgi complexes, microtubules/microfilaments, and nuclei.

WE ARE WHAT WE EAT

STANDARDS OF HEALTH AND NUTRITIONAL DELIVERY

The public has been aware of minimum daily requirements based upon scientific knowledge from the late 1800s to early 1900s. This knowledge is based upon the amount of minerals and vitamins in cells and a determination of what is essential based upon biochemical reactions. However, ingesting the required amount of vitamins and minerals every day is not the same as the cells absorbing these materials.

It need hardly be argued that vitamins and minerals are essential. It has been known since ancient times that human health is dependent on diet. Until recent times, the impact of diet upon health was a process of trial and error. In the more recent history of Western Europe, the first "public" application of knowledge acquired in such a way was the prevention of scurvy at sea. In the first half of the

18th century, it was established through careful observation that scurvy was due to a lack of fresh food, particularly fruit and vegetables, and could be prevented. The publication in 1753 of Lind's treatise on the prevention of scurvy could be regarded as the landmark inauguration of the history of dietary standards.

By 1796, the Royal Navy was providing lemon juice—known as "lime juice"—to its sailors: the term "limey," a slang nickname for the British which originally referred to British sailors, is derived from "lime-juicer," referring to the Royal Navy and the mercantile fleet practice of supplying lemon juice to British sailors to prevent scurvy. The first formal action to institute dietary recommendations was the passage of the British Merchant Seaman's Act in Britain in 1835, by which the provision of lemon juice to prevent scurvy was made compulsory in the rations of the mercantile service.

At the time, nobody knew why fresh fruits and vegetables prevented scurvy. By the mid 19th century, deficiency diseases were correctly diagnosed, yet could not be explained. During the next 50 years, mainly individual scientists or physicians put several other dietary recommendations in place. Most of these prescriptions were based on the observed protein and energy intakes of working people. All the recommendations proposed prior to the early part of the 20th century, except that for citrus juice for sailors, dealt only with energy sources and protein. The nutritional importance of other components of foods in the maintenance of health was recognized only at the beginning of the 1900s.

By the1930s, dietary standards were proposed in connection with efforts to alleviate the deprivation caused by the economic depression by a committee of the British Medical Association.

The purpose of dietary standards shows an evolution from prevention of scurvy (1753), starvation diseases (1862), feeding the army and the nation (1918), maintaining health and working capacity (1933), joining health and agriculture (1935), to maintaining public health (1941).

The USA National Nutrition Conference for Defense (1941) was responsible through the National Research Council for a new charter of requirements formulated on a new level.

To help people better understand the minimum and maximum doses for supplements, the Institute of Medicine has established some guidelines.

The **RDA (recommended dietary allowance)** and the **AI (adequate intake)** are the amounts of a vitamin or mineral needed to maintain health and avoid nutritional deficiencies, tailored to women, men, and specific age groups.

The **UL (tolerable upper intake level)** is the maximum amount of daily vitamins and minerals that can be safely taken without risking an overdose or serious side effects. For certain nutrients, the higher you go above the UL, the greater the chance of having problems.

Separate from the RDA and the UL, the FDA uses a different measurement of nutritional intake.

The **DV (Daily Value)** is the only measurement you'll find on food and supplement labels. That's because space is limited, and there's a need for one single reference number. That number is the amount of a vitamin or nutrient that a person should get for optimum health from a two-thousand-calories-a-day diet. The DV is sometimes the same as the RDA and sometimes not.

Although the details may be different, remember that the RDA and DV are both designed to help us get the nutrients we need to prevent disease and avoid problems caused by malnutrition.

But many people take higher doses of specific supplements in the hopes of gaining other health benefits, like added protection against illness or treatment of disease.

Is taking doses higher than the RDA or DV safe? For many vitamins and minerals, the answer is yes. In some cases, doctors even recommend it. However, as will be discussed later in this book, taking higher doses of vitamins and minerals does not guarantee the absorption, indeed, you may be just throwing the nutrients down the drain at an added expense to you. Without absorption there is no benefit to taking vitamins and minerals.

How they're evaluated:

Recommended Dietary Allowances, prepared by the Food and Nutrition Board of the National Academy of Sciences, have been around for over 50 years, with periodic updates. (Institute of Medicine (US) Food and Nutrition Board, 1998)

The dietary requirement for a micronutrient is defined as an intake level that meets a specified criterion for adequacy, thereby minimizing risk of nutrient deficit or excess. These criteria cover a gradient of biological effects related to a range of nutrient intakes that, at the extremes, include the intake required to prevent death associated with nutrient deficit or excess (WHO FAO 2004).

HEALTH THROUGH GOOD NUTRITION

There is no doubt that nutrient deficiencies and excesses can influence disease states. A number of diseases are associated with mineral deficiencies or impaired metabolism of minerals. Supplementation with minerals has improved the nutritional status and lowered disease risk and progression factors among patients with arthritis, diabetes, cancer, anorexia, and hypertension.

A new study published in the *Annals of Internal Medicine* finds that women in their fifties who eat a Mediterranean-style diet rich in fish, nuts, vegetables, and fruit were about 40 percent more likely to reach the later decades without developing chronic diseases and memory or physical problems, compared to women who didn't eat as well (Aubrey, 2013).

Researchers tracked the dietary habits and lifestyles of more than ten thousand women, beginning in late middle age. Every two years, the women filled out detailed surveys describing their diets. Over the next fifteen years, researchers kept track of which women developed diseases such as Parkinson's, cancer, and lung and pulmonary disease. The women were also given various memory tests and were evaluated for physical function and their abilities to move around and stay active. The results of the research suggests that a healthy diet can help improve multiple aspects of health and can directly affect the ability of people to function when they get older.

How we eat has a direct impact on our bodies down to the cells. Our diets provide fuel for each and every cell in our bodies. When we do not receive enough nutritive sustenance, cells become weakened and pathogens can take control of the cell.

With cells in an already-weakened state, it further impacts the body's ability to absorb nutrients, even when proper nutrition is presented to the cells. This includes people who live in starvation-stricken nations. While food relief may be sent to them, the nutrition may not be able to be fully absorbed adequately due to the declined health status of the population. Furthermore, this same stress factor affects agricultural crops in the absorption of nutrients and is exacerbated in nutrient poor soil that deepens the severity of the populations' health status in poor countries.

Is there a way to improve delivery of nutrients in food and supplements into cell absorption?

Chapter 2. Traditional Cell Metabolism & Immunology

What doesn't kill us makes us stronger.

Cellular metabolism is the set of biochemical processes by which energy is either created or used in the cell. Energy resources in animal cells are regulated by the mitochondrion and the chloroplast.

Immunology is the biological mechanism that creates the search and destroy components for neutralizing disease-causing agents (also known as pathogens, i.e., bacteria, viruses, fungi, worms, etc.) within a larger organism.

Standard metabolic rates are determined in general by only three factors: temperature, mass, and genetic predisposition.

The energy contained within molecules is defined by their chemical bond structure and is called potential energy. The breakage of those chemical bonds is one way that living cells harness this energy to perform cellular functions.

Cell Metabolism in Response to Extracellular and Intracellular Conditions Determining Pathogenicity

Cells are active participants in their environment, constantly adjusting their structure and function to accommodate changing demands internally, by extracellular stresses, and other mechanisms. Cells tend to maintain their intracellular milieu within a fairly narrow range of physiologic parameters to maintain normal homeostasis. As cells encounter physiologic stresses or pathologic stimuli, they can undergo adaptation, achieving a new steady state and preserving viability and function. The principal adaptive responses of a cell are standard growth, slow growth (disease state), fast growth (increased metabolic state), and abnormal growth (cancer).

If the adaptive capability of a cell is exceeded or if the external stress is inherently harmful, cell injury develops. Within certain limits, cell injury is reversible, and the cell can return to a stable baseline; however, severe or persistent stress results in irreversible injury and death of the affected cells. Cell death is one of the most crucial events in the evolution of disease in any tissue or organ. Terminal results can be from diverse causes, including ischemia (lack of blood flow), infections, toxins, and immune reactions. Cell death is also a normal and essential process in promotion of the development of organs, and the maintenance of homeostasis.

Cell Health and Mitochondria -Mitochondrial Alterations
Mitochondrial dysfunction plays an important role in acute cell injury and death. In some nonlethal disease conditions, however, there may be alterations in the number, size, shape, and presumably function of mitochondria within the cell. For example, in cellular hypertrophy (increased growth) there is an increase in the number of mitochondria in cells; conversely, mitochondria decrease in number during cellular atrophy (decreased growth). Mitochondria may assume extremely large and abnormal shapes (mega-mitochondria), as seen in hepatocytes (liver cells) in various nutritional deficiencies and alcoholic liver disease. In certain inherited metabolic diseases of skeletal muscle, the mitochondrial metabolic changes are associated with increased numbers of unusually larger mitochondria containing abnormal internal structures.

Cell Injury

Now that we have discussed the causes of cell injury and necrosis and their morphologic and functional correlates, we next consider in more detail the molecular basis of cell injury, and then illustrate the important principles with a few selected examples of common types of injury. The biochemical mechanisms linking any given injury with the resulting cellular and tissue manifestations are complex, interconnected, and tightly interwoven with many intracellular metabolic pathways. It is therefore often difficult to pinpoint specific molecular alterations caused by a particular action.

General principles relevant to cell injury:
• The cellular response to injurious stimuli depends on the type of injury, its duration, and its severity. Thus, low doses of toxins or a brief duration of cellular suppression may lead to reversible cell injury, whereas larger toxin doses or longer suppressive intervals may result in irreversible injury or, even cell death.
• The consequences of an injurious stimulus depend on the type, status, adaptability, and genetic makeup of the affected cell. The same type of injurious action may have vastly different outcomes depending on the cell type; thus, striated skeletal muscle in the leg accommodates complete ischemia (restriction of blood flow) for two to three hours without irreversible injury, whereas cardiac muscle dies after only twenty to thirty minutes of deprivation. The nutritional (or hormonal) status can also be important; clearly, a glycogen-replete hepatocyte will

tolerate ischemia much better than one that has just burned its last glucose molecule. Genetically determined diversity in metabolic pathways can also be important. For instance, when exposed to the same dose of a toxin, individuals who inherit variants in genes encoding cytochrome P-450 may catabolize the toxin at different rates, leading to different outcomes. Much effort is now directed toward understanding the role of genetics in responses to drugs and toxins and in disease susceptibility. The study of such interactions is called *pharmacogenomics*.
• Cell injury results from functional and biochemical abnormalities in one or more of several essential cellular components. The most important targets of injurious stimuli are (1) mitochondria, the sites of ATP generation; (2) cell membranes, on which the ionic and osmotic homeostasis of the cell and its organelles depends; (3) protein synthesis; (4) the cell membrane; and (5) the genetic apparatus of the cell.

Subcellular Delivery
Currently drug delivery to subcellular compartments is achieved by designing or identifying drugs that are able to permeate the membrane, which diffuse through intestinal and target cell membranes to pervade the entire cell. Linkage of the drug to a lipid promotes membrane absorption. Endosomes moderate cell surface receptors, which mediate endocytosis for cell entry. The endoplasmic reticulum and the Golgi complex control the delivery of conjugated antigens or other proteins. Cytosolic (inside the cell) delivery is done through conjugation with cell-penetrating peptides. The nucleus moderates the delivery of genes. The cell membrane is an important site for cellular signaling events, and many proteins of therapeutic interest are localized in this point. This system needs to be enhanced and modified to improve delivery of therapeutic agents (Rajendran et al., 2010).

The endocytic route engages mainly receptor–ligand complexes. Upon binding of the nutrient or ligand to its cognate receptor transmembrane receptors engage adaptor proteins to initiate the formation of coated pits. The invaginated pits are released into the cytoplasm as vesicles, aided by a small GTPase called dynamin that facilitates the fission process. After delivery to early (sorting) endosomes, the endocytosed cargo is recycled, sorted for degradation or delivered to the Golgi complex.

Targeting to early endosomes which have lower pH than the extracellular environment, serve as sorting stations for endocytosed proteins. The unique pH environment of the endosomes regulates the activity of endosome-specific enzymes and is used by pH dependent pore forming toxins to disrupt the endosomal membrane. The low pH of the endosomal lumen also allows the design of pH dependent prodrugs against therapeutic targets in diseases such as cancer and Alzheimer's disease. (Rajendran, 2010)

Lysosomal storage diseases in which accumulation of undigested metabolites often results in neurological symptoms arise owing to mutations that lead to defective localization or trafficking of lysosomal hydrolases to lysosomes from the Endoplasmic Reticulum or Golgi complex.

The cytoplasm hosts various metabolic, signaling and pathogenic processes that are targets for several diseases. Viruses deliver their genome to the cytosol by fusion of their envelopes at the plasma membrane or in endosomes. Post-transcriptional control mechanisms, such as those mediated by microRNA and small interfering RNA (siRNA), occur in the cytoplasm, and therapeutic siRNAs have to be targeted to this subcellular compartment. To target drugs to the cytosol and avoid lysosomal degradation, several strategies have been devised. These involve the use of cell-penetrating peptides (CPP) that permeate through the plasma membrane bilayer and release the drug directly into the cytosol; pH responsive carriers that dispense the drug into the cytosol from the endosomes; and endosome disrupting agents that aid in the release of drugs into the cytosol.

Drug Targeting to Mitochondria

Drugs reaching the cytosol need to be further targeted if their targets reside in membrane-bound compartments that are not accessible from the surface by endocytic routes. Mitochondria serve as hotspots for targeted therapy both in host cells and in parasites. In host cells, mitochondrial proteins such as B cell lymphoma family proteins serve as anticancer targets. Inhibiting the electron transfer chain or the redox system in parasite mitochondria is a successful antimicrobial approach. Furthermore, dysfunction in mitochondria has been observed in several neurodegenerative diseases such as Parkinson's disease, Alzheimer's disease, and amyotrophic lateral sclerosis (Rajendran et al., 2010).

Receptor endocytosis is the process by which cells absorb materials—such as a drug attached to folic acid—that have been captured at special sites, called receptors, on the cell surface. The compound is then broken down and processed, releasing the drug. One of the key mechanisms of this breakdown is disulfide reduction, which involves the breaking of chemical bonds.

Innate Immune System
The innate immune system is the first line of defense for the body. It is also known as the nonspecific immune system. It is composed of the cells and mechanisms that defend the body from infection by other organisms, recognizing and responding to pathogens in a generic way, but unlike the adaptive immune system (which is only found in vertebrates), it does not give protection for an extended period of time. Innate immune systems provide immediate defense against infection and are found in all classes of plant and animal life.

HOW THE IMMUNE SYSTEM WORKS

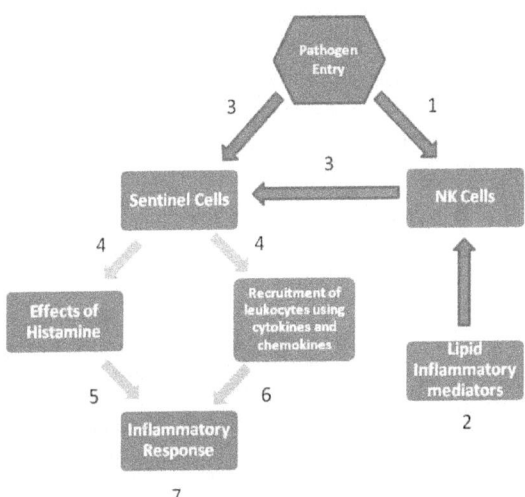

The major functions of the vertebrate innate immune system include (Wikipedia, 2013):

- (1: Pathogen entry into NK Cells): Recruiting immune cells to sites of infection, through the production of chemical factors, including specialized chemical mediators, called cytokines (2: Lipid Inflammatory Mediators);

- Activation of the complement cascade to identify bacteria, activate cells (3: Pathogen entry into Sentinel cells), and to promote clearance of dead cells or antibody complexes (4: Recruitment of leukocytes using cytokines and chemokines);

- The identification and removal of foreign substances present in organs, tissues, and blood and lymph, by specialized white blood cells (5: Effects of Histamine on Inflammatory Response);

- Activation of the adaptive immune system through a process known as antigen presentation (6: Recruitment of leukocytes using cytokines and chemokines upon Inflammatory Response);

- Acting as a physical and chemical barrier to infectious agents (7: Inflammatory response).

Immune cells are functionally regulated by key signaling pathways, which mediate immune function by enabling a response to various stimuli. This response must be carefully moderated in order to avoid hyper-responsiveness or inadequacy in the presence of foreign antigens.

Metabolism is also coordinated at the cellular level. Cells integrate signals from their environment and adjust their chemical reactions to adapt to those signals. Cell-signaling pathways often lead to the activation of protein kinases—enzymes that bond a phosphate group to target proteins.

Effects of Stress on Immunity

Animals have to endure many stressors in their natural environments. For example, they experience food shortages, dwell in areas where predator or parasite densities are high, engage in conflicts with neighbors or group members, and face fluctuations in food and water availability and temperature. Although individuals can often predict when stressors will occur (e.g., more stressors generally in winter than summer), predictions about the intensity or duration of individual stressors are generally not possible (Martin et al., 2011).

In vertebrates, an important mechanism for coping with stressors begins with adrenally-derived glucocorticoid hormones: corticosterone in amphibians, reptiles, and birds, or cortisol in fish and many mammals. These molecules drive gluconeogenesis, suppress reproductive processes, alter movement and feeding rates, impact immune functions, and generally help an individual enter a "state of emergency" when an environmental stressor induces their release. (Martin et al, 2011)

Physicians have long known of the immunosuppressive effects of glucocorticoids, and have used synthetic glucocorticoids to suppress immune functions and assuage the symptoms of, or complications from, inflammatory disorders (e.g., asthma, arthritis, etc.). Whereas all immune functions are eventually suppressed by glucocorticoids, adaptive immune defenses are most sensitive. After only a few days of glucocorticoid elevation, T and B cells can be induced to self-destruct. Innate immune cells, and especially macrophages, can be quite resistant to glucocorticoids however, and in some cases, their resistance can increase in response to chronic glucocortoid or stressor exposure. (Martin et al., 2011)

Most research on glucocorticoid effects on immune system function has focused on suppressive effects, not surprisingly given many of the above effects. However, glucocorticoids have complex effects on immune functions, an observation consistent with an emerging theme in ecology that hosts can either resist or tolerate parasites. Resistance involves mechanisms that limit parasite burden, whereas tolerance involves mechanisms that limit the impacts of a given burden on reproductive fitness or performance. It is important to distinguish between these mechanisms because they impact both the persistence and emergence of disease as well as the evolution of virulence differently. For these reasons, it may be important to determine whether and how stress hormones impact tolerance. Several indirect lines of evidence indicate that glucocorticoids mediate tolerance (e.g., release of the cytokine, interleukin-10). More importantly, once resistance barriers are breached, tolerance mechanisms must be activated. As glucocorticoids can reduce resistance (i.e., immunosuppression), they can also foster tolerance.

The author has done several early studies looking at environmental stress on mice showing that blood levels of cortisol rise during stress. Swimming stress seems to significantly slow tumor progression and extend the lifespan of mice with cancer as compared to controls. When temperature and humidity stresses were applied there was no anti-tumor or decreased tumor growth benefit. This tends to indicate that increased glucocorticoid synthesis may aide longevity. (Sonnenschein, 1979)

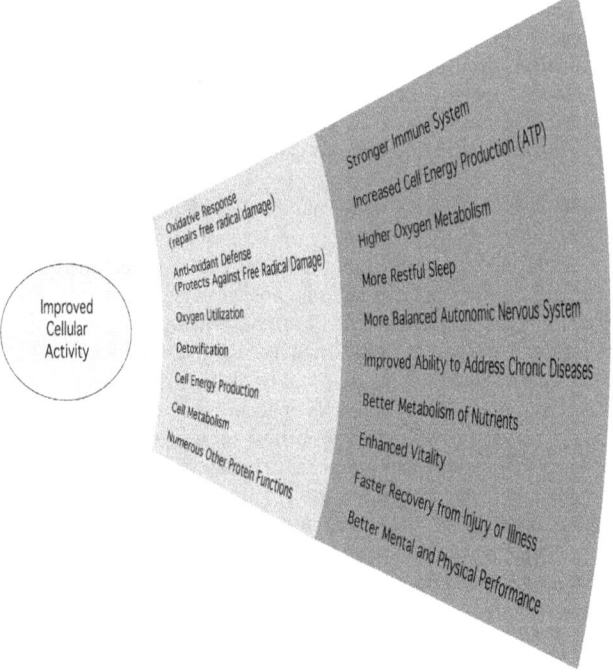

Immune Redistribution

A dominant focus in stress-coping research has been the effects of acute versus chronic stressors on performance and fitness, including immune functions. As above, chronic stressors tend to suppress immune functions, although immune cells and tissues vary in their sensitivity to stressors and stress hormones. Interestingly though, acute stressors often enhance immune functions as a result of glucocorticoid-immune interactions. These effects include increased memory of antigens (and other products), but the best-studied effects are enhancements of skin inflammatory responses and immune cell influx to wounds. These latter effects are especially relevant for wild animals, because wounds are a common consequence of failed predation attempts and territorial conflicts, two of the most common stressors wild animals experience. These observations led to the hypothesis that acute stressor induced immune enhancement might include immune redistribution. In support of this hypothesis, brief restraint of domesticated rodents prior to the induction of a skin inflammatory response enhanced both the physical size of the immune response and the number of immune cells entering the skin. (Martin et al., 2011)

Similar experiments have not been successfully performed in wild animals, most likely because it is difficult to conduct such studies on animals that perceive handling by humans, and housing in captivity, as predation events. For example, while attempting to determine whether acute stressors enhanced immune function in the skin of wild house sparrows, captivity itself was found to impact immune responses. After a couple of days in captivity, the type and abundance of immune cells infiltrating the skin began to change; after four weeks in captivity, the makeup of the immune cells entering the skin was altogether different than that of a wild-caught bird. Subsequent studies have indicated that glucocorticoid regulation breaks down over captivity in house sparrows: baseline levels remain very high, release in response to stressors no longer occurs, and hormone receptor expression in the brain changes after a month in what are perceived to be benign, controlled lab conditions. (Martin et al., 2011)

Chapter 3. New Mechanisms for Understanding Cell Metabolism

We React to Our Environment

The cell membrane is made up of chemicals and liquids that create a barrier for the inside as well as the outside of the cell. The cell wall requires energy for its maintenance. Based upon those needs, the cell wall gives messages to organelles on what to produce, including when the cell needs to divide. Therefore, the new mechanism for understanding cell metabolism is to recognize the cell wall's responsibility for regulating a cell's metabolism rather than the nucleus.

It is really the cell wall that controls a cell's capacity for accepting or rejecting nutrients. There are several ways for nutrients and other chemical compounds to cross through the cell's membrane.

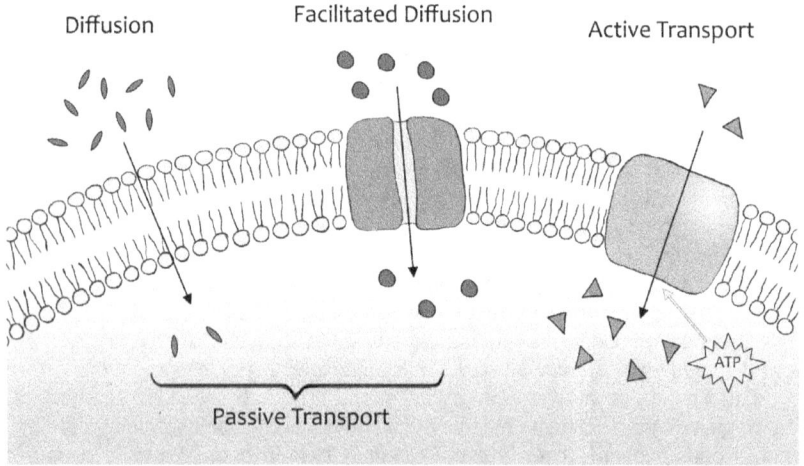

1. Passive Transport. Cell transport utilizing a concentration gradient for the nutrient across the membrane. Passive transport can be further divided into:
   a. Diffusion. In order for molecules to simply diffuse across a membrane, they must either be quite small so as to enter membrane pores, go via the paracellular

route, or be soluble in the lipid membrane. Water is a good example of a small molecule, as are the gases and ethanol. Many lipids are soluble in the lipid bilayer and are transported by simple diffusion.

b. Facilitated Diffusion or transport that is facilitated by a transport protein, the driving force is still the concentration gradient. Glucose and amino acids also use this mechanism. Diffusion is defined as the net motion of a substance from an area of high concentration to an area of low concentration, also known as 'moving down a concentration gradient.

Factors that affect diffusion:
- How steep the concentration gradient is
- Temperature
- Surface area
- Type of molecule

Molecules and ions that are small enough can cross membranes easily, regardless of polarity, but large polar molecules such as glucose cannot diffuse through a cell membrane. They can only pass through hydrophilic protein channels—this process is known as **facilitated diffusion.** (Wikibooks, 2013)

There is considerable evidence that the efficiency of drugs could be enhanced by modifications that increase their affinity for the plasma membrane. For example, the membrane affinity of peptide hormones determines their biological activity. Membrane anchoring, through either lipid or protein conjugation, increases the concentration of the drug at the target membrane and confines the drug to subdomains therein, thereby increasing the effective concentration at the membrane and decreasing the half maximal inhibitory concentration of the compound. Membrane anchoring also reduces the dimensionality of a drug, increases the half-life of the compound and/or enables efficient inhibition of conformation specific events at the membrane.

The Role of the Inflammation Process

Inflammation is the body's immunological response to bodily injury. Acute inflammation is the localized response following a trauma or an infection and can result in pain, heat, swelling, and redness at the site of the injury. Inflammation may also involve loss of function of the involved tissues. However, if inflammation persists for a prolonged period of time, the inflammation becomes chronic as the result of a viral or microbial infection, environmental antigen (e.g., pollen), autoimmune reaction, or persistent activation of inflammatory molecules (Drake, 2013).

The inflammation process involves a ripple effect of molecular and cellular signals that alter physiological responses, ultimately resulting in pain, heat, swelling, and redness. At the site of the injury, cells release molecular signals that cause the dilation of blood vessels, increased blood flow, increased vascular permeability, a discharge of fluids containing proteins such as antibodies, and invasion by white blood cells.

When cells are exposed to an osmotic change caused by BOOSTER™, it's like getting a slap in the cellular face. To cells, it's a nasty shock. To counteract it, cells go into overdrive. It's similar to blood rushing to someone's face after the unpleasant stimulus of a slap. When cells are put back into normal conditions, instead of relaxing, they retain high metabolic activity as they mature. BOOSTER™ is like a series of light pats on the cheek, to keep the color up.

BOOSTER™ stimulates increased cell action by creating a mini-inflammatory response. Looking at this through an electron microscope, we see increased mitochondria, Golgi complexes and endoplasmic reticulum. These are the organelle systems for energy and immunity and cellular metabolism pathways for pathogen recognition for the immune response. Being that BOOSTER™ increases these organelles, we believe that this also is the mechanical representation for the improved immune responses we see in fish, invertebrates, and humans, which have been tested with BOOSTER™ technology.

Chapter 4. New Ideas Regarding Cell Nutrition

The cell membrane is the welcome mat to everything and everybody. Whatever the cell wall is exposed to, some things get welcomed in, and some things are blocked from entering. There needs to be an understanding about system metabolism, which will then affect the cell maintenance directed by the nucleus.

The cell membrane allows the absorption of all nutrition and has the responsibility to create receptivity based upon the nutritional status of cell. The chemical reactions of metabolism are organized into metabolic pathways, in which one chemical is transformed into another by a sequence of enzymes. Enzymes are crucial to metabolism and allow the fine regulation of metabolic pathways to maintain a constant set of conditions in response to changes in the cell's environment, a process known as *homeostasis*.

Amino acids are absorbed through the wall of the small intestine into the bloodstream and distributed throughout the body to repair injuries and replace dying cells.

Once nutrients are in the bloodstream, they will be carried to every cell of the body, but once delivered, each cell must have mechanisms to absorb the nutrients from the blood or interstitial fluid. The membrane barrier that exists in the intestine exists in every cell.

It has been understood for decades that the nucleus controls all cell functions and that mitochondria control energy production for keeping the cell alive. A healthy cell is one that maintains homeostasis. If a cell is not in homeostasis, it will block absorption.

What we know is when we apply BOOSTER™ to vitamins, the cells absorb proportionately up to ten times the dose. When patients take the BOOSTER™-treated vitamins, they are healthier. When cosmetics are applied with BOOSTER™, a more successful treatment follows. When fish are treated with the saline process, they grow faster and more resistant to pathogens and have increased hormone, glycogen (energy substance), and fatty-acid production. Therefore, cellular activity is controlled by the outside of the cell, which creates organelle responses at the cellular level, which are in turn delivered to the nucleus, which is a receptor for this transitory information. The nucleus in response can tell the cell to divide or further direct organelle actions and dispositions according to the external modulation of the cell wall.

Chapter 5. Updating Cellular Immunology

As the cell membrane is stimulated, it also causes the organelles that modulate immunity to be stimulated in their efficiency for reaction to pathogens.

As multivitamins are injested into the body, a portion of those nutrients actually make it into the cell, thereby energizing the cell and, ultimately, our bodies. The same situation exists when we take an over-the-counter drug or a prescription drug. Nutraceutical and pharmaceutical companies are always in pursuit of efficient pathways that enable their products to get into the cell. The more product that gets into the cell, the more effective the product will be for the consumer. BOOSTER™ is the result of our research and significantly aides the absorption of an active ingredient.

Cellular processes form fundamental systems that involve complicated cascades of biochemical reactions and signaling pathways. For proper cell function, these processes are required to be tightly controlled. Deregulation of any element of these pathways, from over- or under-activity of an enzyme, increase or decrease in the level of a protein, to under- or overexpression of an ion channel, can lead to a vast array of human pathologies. Some other related data are:

Sodium, in association with serum albumin, is essential for maintaining blood volume. An albumin is a protein that is soluble in water and also in salt solutions. Without adequate sodium, the serum albumin is unable to keep water from leaving the blood and entering the tissues. The tissues swell as the volume of blood is reduced.

A lack of sodium slows metabolism, lowers carbon dioxide production, and creates inflammation, stress, and deterioration. On the other hand, sodium stimulates energy metabolism, increases carbon dioxide production, and protects against inflammation and other negative stress reactions.

Hypertonic solutions contain two times to eight times more sodium than normal can be used to resuscitate people and animals after injury. Rather than just increasing the amount of blood in the circulatory system, the hypertonic sodium solution restores cellular energy production, causing the increase of oxygen consumption and heat production while reducing free radical production. Hypertonic sodium solutions also improve the functioning of the heart muscle and reduce inflammation, blood vessel penetration or saturation, and swelling of cells.

Seawater, which is hypertonic to our tissues, has often been used for treating wounds, and highly concentrated salt solutions have been found effective for accelerating wound healing (Mangete et al., 1992).

A low-sodium diet accelerates the decrease in body heat production that normally occurs with aging, lowering the metabolic rate, increasing the fat content of the body, and slowing activity of fat-synthesizing enzymes.

Cellular Adaptations to Stress
• *Hypertrophy:* increased cell size, often in response to increased workload; induced by mechanical stress and by growth factors; occurs in tissues incapable of cell division
• *Hyperplasia:* increased cell numbers in response to hormones and other growth factors; occurs in tissues whose cells are able to divide
• *Atrophy:* decreased cell size, as a result of decreased nutrient supply or disuse; associated with decreased synthesis and increased breakdown of cellular organelles
• *Metaplasia:* change in phenotype of differentiated cells, often a response to chronic irritation that makes cells better able to withstand the stress; usually induced by altered differentiation pathway of tissue stem cells; may result in reduced functions or increased propensity for malignant transformation.

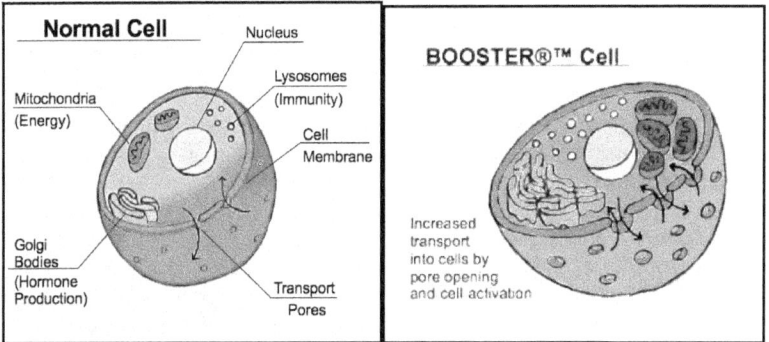

How BOOSTER™ Works

BOOSTER™ works through utilization of a transport effect as solution changes by molecular proportions. With the addition of sodium (for which the cell membrane has a particular resting concentration), additional sodium forces the pores and channels to open to allow solution exchange from the inside of the cell to the outside by pressurizing water to escape the cell to produce homeostasis, physically opening the pores and channels. As the outside solution changes, the pores/channels can be closed to process larger molecules. This is a transport affected by solution changes. Larger pore/channel openings allow a subsequent larger molecule passage and/or cellular incorporation depending on molecule concentration of the solution and its constitution.

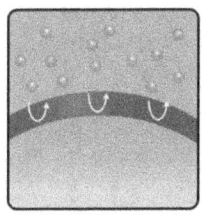 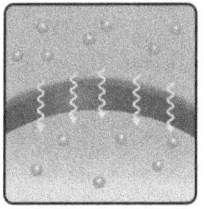

No BOOSTER™   **With BOOSTER™**

Without BOOSTER™, the cell retains its normal hydration and physical properties of resistance including osmotic regulation and only water and small, water-soluble molecules such as sodium, glucose, potassium, and other ions can transport through the cell membrane.

Chapter 6. Delivery of Active Ingredients

What we eat, the medicines we take, and the cosmetics we spread on our skin all have active ingredients. However, these ingredients are not, in general, correctly balanced for efficient absorption.

The cell membrane only allows particles up to a particular size to enter. Most formulations of cosmetic, nutritional, and medicinal products don't consider the molecular base of the active ingredients to be applied with their homeostatic states. Because of this, it is suggested that many products need to undergo changes with BOOSTER™ and GroFish™ technology to improve the effectiveness of active ingredient delivery.

Permeability (P) of molecules across a membrane can be expressed as:

$$P = \frac{KD}{\Delta x}$$

where K is the partition coefficient, D is the diffusion coefficient, and Δx is the thickness of the cell membrane. The diffusion coefficient (D) is a measure of the rate of entry into the cytoplasm depending on the molecular weight or size of a molecule. K is a measure of the solubility of the substance in lipids. A low value of K describes a molecule like water that is not soluble in lipid.

To aid in a molecule's permeability, a linker, which is usually an oligomer, is introduced to connect the active pharmacophore to the lipid anchor. Direct conjugation of the drug to the lipid molecule might hinder the interaction of the drug with its intended target by causing steric hindrance or by placing the drug too close to the lipid bilayer. Oligo (ethylene glycol) or oligoamides can be used as backbone structures for linkers. The linker lengths could be adjusted to optimize accessibility to the target molecule. In some cases, the optimal length of the linker could be designed by analyzing the drug–target interaction site and the distance of this interaction site from the bilayer. Linkers also provide space to introduce additional modifications, such as sites for enzymatic cleavage, pH-dependent cleavage moieties, disulphide bonds to modulate glutathione-dependent reduction and consequently the liberation of linked molecules. Such linkers are crucial for the design of lipid-linked prodrugs. (Rajendran et al., 2010)

There is considerable evidence that the efficiency of these drugs could be enhanced by modifications that increase their affinity for the plasma membrane. For example, the membrane affinity of peptide hormones determines their biological activity. Membrane anchoring, through either lipid or protein conjugation, increases the concentration of the drug at the target membrane and confines the drug to subdomains therein, thereby increasing the effective concentration at the membrane and decreasing the half maximal inhibitory concentration of the compound. Membrane anchoring also reduces the dimensionality of a drug, increases the half-life of the compound and/or enables efficient inhibition of conformation specific events at the membrane.

Delivery of Active Ingredients

Can we improve drug specificity by increasing its concentration in the cellular compartment in which the drug exerts its action?

INDEPENDENT RESEARCH REPORT ON BOOSTER™

Robust Vitamin D₃ Absorption

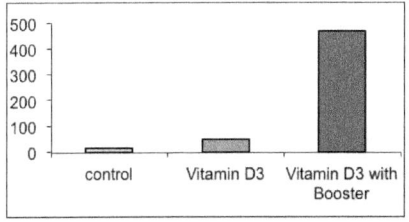

Independent laboratory analysis (GVK, Hyderabad, India) of the efficacy of BOOSTER™ has been conducted. Male mice were administered vitamin D_3 along with a control or a BOOSTER™-supplemented diet. The objective of this study was to determine the urine concentrations of vitamin D_3 in mice after oral administration of vitamin D_3 incorporated in the diet at 25,000 IU. The BOOSTER™-treated urine concentration of vitamin D_3 was 9.8 times higher than the control group. Therefore, BOOSTER™ very significantly increased the absorption of vitamin D_3 in this mammalian model.

Source: Animal Facility and Bioanalytical and Pharmacokinetic Analysis Facility, GVK Biosciences Pvt. Ltd. Biology Division, 28 A, IDA, Nacharam, Hyderabad 500 079 India.

BOOSTER™ and GroFish™: Mechanisms of Action

How It Works: Large Molecule Intercellular Induction

Ionic levels are raised; the cell excretes fluids to gain equilibrium. The pores in this process are opened, and large molecules that are placed outside the cell are absorbed through the pores. Homeostasis is achieved and the pores are sealed, locking large molecules inside the cell, in its interstitial fluid, effectively injecting the large molecules into the cell without using a needle.

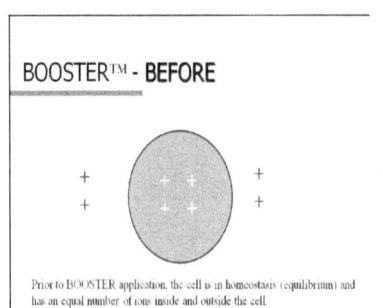

BOOSTER™ - **BEFORE**

Prior to BOOSTER application, the cell is in homeostasis (equilibrium) and has an equal number of ions inside and outside the cell.

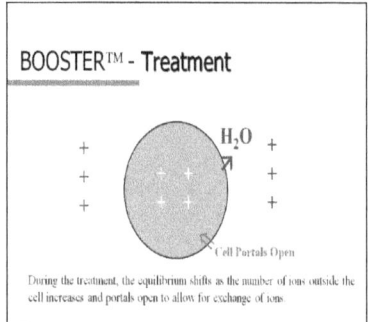

BOOSTER™ - **Treatment**

During the treatment, the equilibrium shifts as the number of ions outside the cell increases and portals open to allow for exchange of ions.

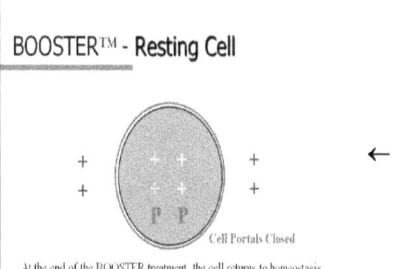

BOOSTER™ - **Resting Cell**

At the end of the BOOSTER treatment, the cell returns to homeostasis (equilibrium) with the Protein (P) remaining within the cell walls.

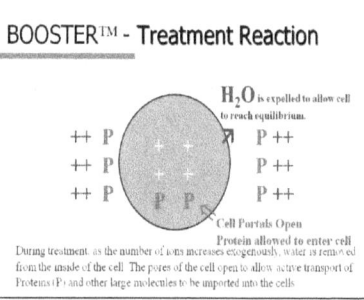

BOOSTER™ - **Treatment Reaction**

During treatment, as the number of ions increases exogenously, water is removed from the inside of the cell. The pores of the cell open to allow active transport of Proteins (P) and other large molecules to be imported into the cells.

Chapter 7. Food Chemistry

What We Eat Is What We Are–Part 2

It is amusing to think about eating food as a chemical process. In this way, our digestive process is really a chemical-processing facility. Disease, lifespan, and health are affected by what we eat. This chapter looks at the mechanisms for food absorption of the whole body and cellular level as well. Some believe food chemistry releases the awakening of the body based on the acid-base influence on blood chemistry.

When we eat such things as bread, meat, and vegetables as well as drink various beverages, they are not in a form that the body can use as nourishment. Our food and drink must be changed into smaller molecules of nutrients before they can be absorbed into the blood and carried to cells throughout the body. Digestion is the process by which food and drink are broken down into their smallest molecular parts so that the body can use them to build and nourish cells and to provide energy.

As long as your nervous system is free of interference and your body has the nutrients it needs, the cells of your body are able to carry out the essential jobs of keeping you alive including—maintaining your heart beating, your lungs breathing, your digestive system digesting food, your eliminative system getting rid of waste, your glands secreting hormones…and everything else necessary to protect you and heal you from injuries and disease.

However, these nutrients must not only get into your body, they must get into the cells of your body. When you read a label identifying the ingredients and compared to the RDA (Recommended Dietary Allowance) standards this is only IF what you eat actually gets absorbed into the cells. One of the reasons nutritional research results are often so inconsistent and conflictive is that many of those studied in the research studies are not receiving consistent cellular uptake due to a number of variables affecting absorption.

- In order for nutrients in supplements and in foods to be effective, they must reach the cells of your body. Otherwise, your body can't use them.
- Generally supplements have an inefficient "delivery system" because the formula of the chemicals does not adequately consider the transmission through the cell membranes and many of the essential nutrients are not allowed to enter the cells without a delivery mechanism combined within the administered product.

Absorption
Absorption is the rate at which and the process by which molecules and elements from the environment enter the interior of the organism via passage across (or around) the lining cells of the gastro-intestinal tract. Absorption occurs all the way from the stomach to the rectum, although the small intestine is where most absorption takes place. Absorptive efficiency for many nutrients, notably iron, calcium and zinc, is governed by homeostatic feedback regulation. When the body stores are too low, the intestine up-regulates the ability with which the intestine takes up the nutrient. When the body reserves are adequate or increased, the gut

down-regulates the nutrient's uptake. At a molecular level, this regulation can be expressed by the control of intraluminal binding ligands, cell surface receptors, intracellular carrier proteins, intracellular storage proteins, or the energetics of the trans-membrane transport system.

Bioavailability refers to the extent to which a nutrient reaches its site of pharmacologic action. For practical purposes, this definition includes the extent to which the nutrient reaches a fluid (e.g., blood) that bathes the site of action and through which the nutrient can readily reach the site of action. In the digestive tract the availability of nutrients is also affected by the amount of solute and solvent available in the tract at one time. The bioavailability of a mineral depends directly on the extent to which the mineral is absorbed and distributed to the site of action. It is necessary to consider the factors that affect absorption in order to determine the relative bioavailability of nutrients in different forms that include time, concentration, and physiologic conditions.

The purpose of **cell transport** is to maintain homeostasis. The different kinds of cell transport are divided into two categories: those that require energy and those that do not.

Passive transport does not require energy. There are three kinds of passive transport. In **diffusion** substances move from high concentrations to low concentrations. In **facilitated diffusion** substances move from high concentrations to low concentrations via **carrier proteins**. Finally, in **osmosis** water moves from high concentrations (of water) to low concentrations.

Active transport requires energy, usually moving substances from low concentrations to high concentrations against the **concentration gradient**.

In **endocytosis**, a form of active transport, the cell engulfs material that is transported.

Factors Affecting Diffusion across a Semipermeable Membrane

- The greater the lipid solubility of the diffusing particle, the more permeable the membrane will be.
- All else being equal, smaller particles will diffuse more rapidly than larger particles.
- Oxygen, water and carbon dioxide rapidly diffuse across the cell membrane.

- Larger hydrophilic uncharged molecules, such as sugars, do not freely diffuse.
- Charged molecules cannot diffuse through lipid bilayer.
- Ion channels and/or specific delivery enhancement are required for charged molecules and larger, uncharged molecule to pass through the cell membranes.

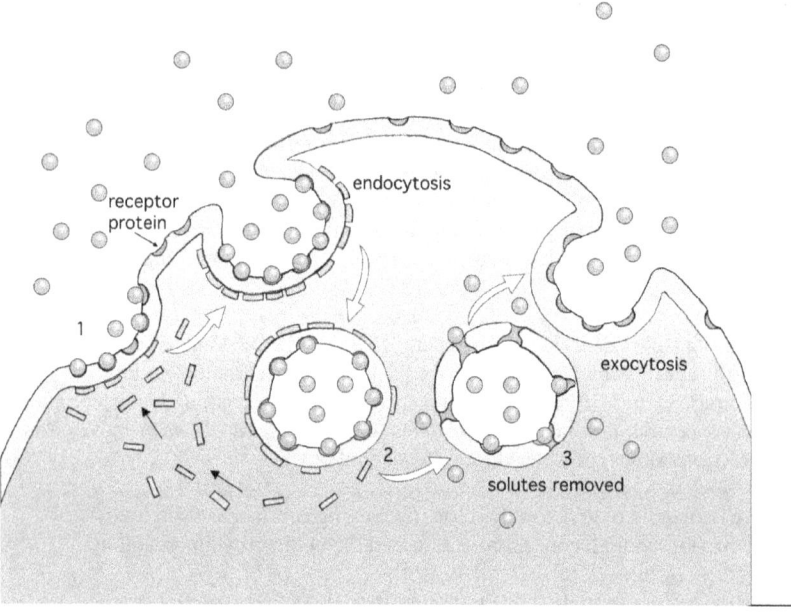

Receptor-mediated endocytosis
(1) The receptors in the coated pits combine only with a solute.
(2) The vesicle that forms is at first coated with a fibrous protein (rectangles), but soon the vesicle loses its coat.
(3) Solutes leave the vesicle.
(4) When exocytosis occurs, membrane and therefore receptors are returned to the plasma membrane.

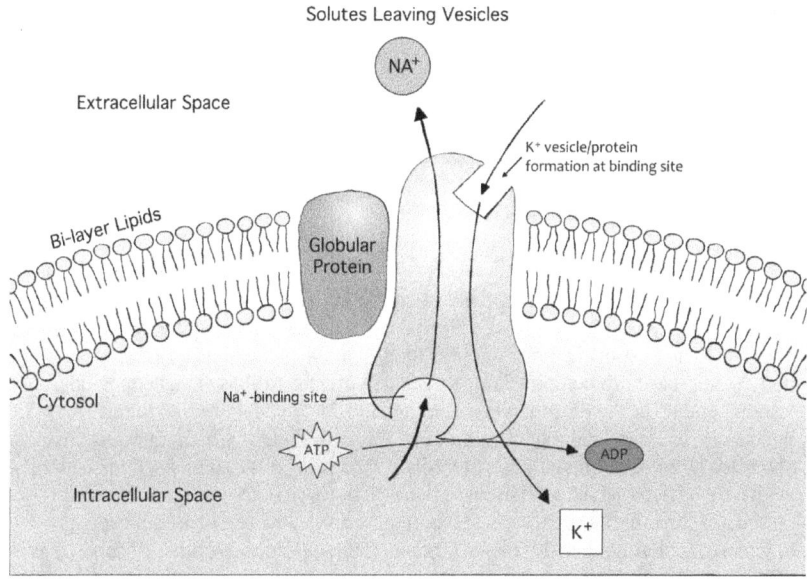

Solutes Leaving Vesicles

□ Cell membranes are more permeable to water than to ions or other solutes, and water moves across them by osmosis from a solution of lower solute concentration to a higher solute concentration.

□ Cells expand or contract when placed in hypotonic or hypertonic solutions, respectively. In order to maintain their normal cytosolic homeostatic osmolality and therefore cell volume, animal cells must export Na^+ and other ions that are transported from the extracellular space into the cytosol.

If an animal cell's nucleus, cell membrane, or organelles fail to function properly, it can cause disease, making it difficult for the organism to carry out life's basic functions.

Without this range of nutrients and phytonutrients, the membranes in your cells can become brittle, develop holes (become leaky), not be able to function properly, and not be protective for your cell's DNA and energy producing machinery. If cellular continuity is not maintained, DNA mutations can develop which can cause the cell to be unable to function, or even to become malignant (cancerous). Damage to the cell integrity can also affect the mitochondrial energy producing machinery leading to an increase in generation of free radicals, causing more damage and destroying your cell's ability to function entirely.

Acid-Base Influence on Blood Chemistry

The foods we eat affect our blood pH or acid-base balance that can be defined as homeostasis of the body fluids at a normal arterial blood pH ranging between 7.37 and 7.43. The chemical composition of food in the diet can have an effect on the body's acid-base production. Components that affect acid-base balance include protein, and a variety of minerals including chloride, phosphorus, sodium, potassium, calcium, and magnesium. In addition, the rate at which nutrients are absorbed in the intestine will alter acid-base balance. Cells and body fluids contain acid-base buffers, which help prevent rapid changes in body-fluid pH over short periods of time, until the kidneys and pulmonary systems can make appropriate adjustments. Eating a well-balanced diet including various pH types of foods may affect overall homeostasis of blood pH.

☐ Changes in pH in blood: arterial blood >7.45 = alkalosis and <7.35 = physiologic acidosis
☐ Body has buffer systems: Bicarbonate and physiologic mechanisms

pH Levels of Food			
Very Acidic Foods	Mildly Acidic Foods	Mildly Alkaline Foods	Very Alkaline Foods
-White Bread	-Meat/Fish	-Fruits	-Asparagus
-Alcohol	-Legumes	-Vegetables	-Cayenne Pepper
-Soda	-Nuts	-Avocados	-Melons
-Sugar	-Dairy	-Almonds	-Kelp

Chapter 8. Setting New Absorption Standards

As discussed in Chapter 1, the standards for daily requirements are set by levels of nutrients based upon metabolic deficits. There needs to be health standards based upon healthy nutrition rather than the bare minimum to prevent disease. This chapter looks at individual vitamins, fatty acids, and minerals recommended for absorption and examines the effects they have on a person's health status.

There is a dire need to set new standards of absorption of nutrients and active ingredients into the body. Not only is the accepted model of absorption incorrect, there are several ways that absorption can be greatly enhanced within the body.

A History of Nutritional Consumption Recommendations
The Recommended Dietary Allowances (RDAs) are quantities of nutrients in the diet that are required to maintain good health in people. RDAs are established by the Food and Nutrition Board of the National Academy of Sciences, and may be revised every few years. A separate RDA value exists for each nutrient. The RDA values refer to the amount of nutrient expected to maintain good health in people. The actual amounts of each nutrient required to maintain good health in specific individuals differ from person to person.

Where possible, the subcommittee established an RDA by first estimating the average physiological requirement for an *absorbed* nutrient. It then adjusted this value by factors to compensate for incomplete utilization and to encompass the variation both in requirements among individuals and in the bioavailability of the nutrient among the food sources. Thus, there is a safety factor in the RDAs for each nutrient, reflecting the state of knowledge concerning the nutrient, its bioavailability, and variations among the U.S. population. It was the intent of the subcommittee that the RDAs be both safe and adequate, but not necessarily the highest or lowest figures that the data might justify. (*Recommended Dietary Allowances*, 10th ed., 1989)

There is not always agreement among experts on the criteria for determining the physiological requirement for a nutrient. The requirement for infants and children may be equated with the amount that will maintain a satisfactory rate of growth and development; for an adult, it may be equated with an amount that will maintain body weight and prevent depletion of the nutrient from the body, as judged by balance studies and maintenance of acceptable blood and tissue concentrations. For certain nutrients, the requirement could be the amount that will prevent failure of a specific function or the development of specific deficiency signs—an amount that may differ greatly from that required to maintain body stores. Thus, designation of the requirement for a given nutrient varies with the criteria chosen. (*Recommended Dietary Allowances*, 10th ed., 1989)

VITAMIN ADMINISTRATION

Effectiveness of liquid vs. solid vitamins

The dissolution rate is important for measuring the absorbability of a mineral. Liquid forms are more digestible. Oral ingestion of a liquid medium, as in colloidal minerals, increases absorbability of minerals.

Water-soluble vitamins need to be consumed daily. They cannot be stored in the body. Fat-soluble vitamins need to be dissolved in fat before they can be transported into the cell. The process requires fat-digesting bile acids in the liver and in body fat, where they're stored until they're needed (much like fat). Fat-soluble vitamins do not need to be consumed every day.

Absorption of vitamins and minerals can be encouraged or thwarted by a variety of factors:

- Mode of administration;
- Pharmaceutical form;
- Size of the dose;
- Site of absorption of the vitamin;
- Competition of other nutrients; and
- Water, Coffee, Tea and Alcohol (The amount of iron absorbed is reduced to one-third if coffee is drunk with a meal)

The size of a molecule can negatively affect absorption rate with other delivery or active-transport mechanisms. Fat-soluble vitamins are protected during digestion by antioxidant nutrients A, C, and E.

Urinary Output = Absorption
Urine is used to extract excess minerals or vitamins as well as blood corpuscles from the body. The urinary organs include the kidneys, ureters, bladder, and urethra. The urinary system works with the other systems of the body to help maintain homeostasis. The nutrients required by our bodies must be dissolved, and then absorbed by the body if they are to be used. The solubility of nutrients is

determined by the molecular properties (e.g., polarity) of the nutrients. It is often useful to quantify the solubility of nutrients, in terms of the amount of the nutrient that is dissolved per unit volume. Although dissolution is a necessary step for nutrients to be absorbed, absorbance depends on more than the solubility of the nutrients. Certain substances in the digestive tract, such as Olestra and phytic acid, can interfere with the absorbance of some nutrients even if the nutrients are dissolved; other substances, such as vitamin D, can enhance nutrient absorption. All of these processes are governed by fundamental chemical properties and principles, such as polarity, molecular structure, intermolecular interactions, thermodynamics, and equilibrium. (Casiday and Frey, 2013)

VITAMIN INFORMATION

Water-Soluble Vitamins

VITAMIN(s) B

Vitamin B(s) are water-soluble and need to be replenished every day, although their absorption works a bit differently. In bound form to proteins release requires a breakdown triggered by stomach acids. Absorption of most of the B vitamins happens in the small intestine, in the ileum.

Vitamin B1-Thiamin

Vitamin B1 is needed for converting food into energy and healthy for skin, hair, muscles and brain. RDA is 1.1 mg and doses above 2.5mg appear to be unabsorbed. Thiamin is commonly found in pork products, soy, squash and watermelon.

Vitamin B2-Riboflavin

Vitamin B2 RDA for men 1.1mg and for women 1.3 mg and is needed for converting food into energy and healthy for skin, hair, muscles and brain. Riboflavin is commonly found in milk products, whole grains and liver.

Vitamin B3-Niacin (nicotinic acid)

Vitamin B3 RDA is 16mg for men and 14mg for women with an upper limit of 35 mg and is needed for a healthy nervous system, blood cells and skin. Niacin is naturally produced in the body from tryptophan with vitamin B6. Niacin is commonly found in poultry, meat, fish, grains, mushrooms, potatoes and peanut butter.

Vitamin B5-Pantothenic acid

Vitamin B5 RDA is 5mg and helps in lipid production including fats, neurotransmitters, hormones, and hemoglobin. Pantothenic acid is commonly found in chicken, grain, tomatoes, broccoli, mushrooms and avocados.

Vitamin B6-Pyridoxine

Vitamin B6 RDA is 1.3mg with upper limit of 100mg with the function of reducing heart disease, helps in the serotonin metabolic pathways regulating activity, sleep, and appetite, cognitive and immune function and red blood cell production. Many people are deficit in this vitamin which is common found in meat, fish, beans, and non-citrus fruits.

Vitamin B12-Cobalamin

Vitamin B12 RDA is 2.4micrograms(mcg) and is not easily absorbed. Cobalamin helps in lowering heart disease, improves health, protects nerve cells, aids memory and helps in red blood cell production. It is found in meat, fish, poultry, cereals and soy milk.

Biotin

Biotin RDA is 30mcg, but very little is known about how much the body absorbs, but is known to be involved in glucose synthesis, fatty acid metabolism, hair and bone growth. It is found in fish, organ meats, whole grains, eggs and soybeans.

VITAMIN C-Ascorbic Acid

Vitamin C RDA is 90mg for men and 75 mg for women with additional amount of 35 mg for smokers and is absorbed in the small intestine (along with most other types of nutrient absorption) with an upper limit of 2000mg per day. Water-soluble vitamins, such as vitamin C, are easily absorbed. Ascorbic acid also aids in the absorption of iron, up to 3 times normal, but inhibits copper. Zinc and manganese absorption is also aided in the presence of vitamin C. Vitamin C is found in fruits and vegetables, especially abundant in citrus. Vitamin C has been shown to help lower the risk for some cancers, and may help prevent cataracts. Vitamin C is a co-factor in many metabolic (biochemical) pathways and as an antioxidant neutralizes free radicals. Vitamin C has long been implicated in bolstering the immune system.

Choline

Choline RDA is 550mg for men and 425mg for women with a upper limit of 3500mg. It is found in milk, eggs, liver and peanuts. The body produces choline and it helps in the production and release of the neurotransmitter acetylcholine for neurologic functions and aids in fat synthesis and deposition.

Folic Acid-Folate

Folate RDA is 400mcg with an upper limit of 1000mcg and is found in grains, asparagus, broccoli, beans, orange and tomato juices, okra, spinach, and turnip greens. Most people are deficient in folate which can lead to severe neurologic pathologies. Folate is vital for new cell creation and plays an important role in child development of the nervous system and has been shown to reduce heart disease and cancer risk in some early studies.

Fat-Soluble Vitamins

VITAMIN A-Retinoic Acid

Retinol as it is also known RDA is 3000 IU(900mcg) for men and 2333IU(700mcg) for women with an upper limit of 10,000IU(3000mcg). Beta carotene is the natural source of Vitamin A and is found in carrots, sweet potatoes, squashes, spinach, mangos and turnip greens. As retinol it is found in beef, eggs, liver, shrimp and milk products. Vitamin A is essential for eye, skin, bone growth and may lower lung cancer risk. Vitamin A is often found in cosmetics, however it is not easily absorbed without a delivery system.

VITAMIN D-Calciferol

Vitamin D3 RDA is 400IU(10mcg) per day with an upper limit of 10,000IU(250mcg). The D3 version is obtained from animals and the D2 version is plant based. The D2 to D3 conversion occurs in the presence of sun, specifically the UV spectrum and allows for calcium and phosphorus absorption in the bone deposition process. The presence of vitamin D_3 is needed to maximize calcium absorption as part of the calciferol process, so it is best to supplement calcium or dolomite with added D. Most people are deficient in vitamin D3 though it is readily supplied in milk, cereals and fatty fish.

VITAMIN E-Alpha-tocopherol

Vitamin E RDA is 15mg with an upper limit of 1000mg. Vitamin E is a potent antioxidant with protects cells from free radicals and damage to vitamin A and lipids in solution. Vitamin E may help prevent prostate cancer and slow progression/onset of Alzheimer's disease. Vitamin E is also used in cosmetics to improve skin conditions, but without a delivery system to get it into the cells, it just acts as an lubricant or filler on the out layer of the skin to which it is applied. Vitamin E is found in vegetable oils, leafy greens, whole grains and nuts.

VITAMIN K-phylloquinone

Vitamin K RDA is 120mcg for men and 90mcg for women, but is also synthesized by intestinal bacteria as its function is to make proteins for blood clotting and is a cofactor in bone and tissue metabolism. Natural sources include kale, Brussels sprouts, spinach, and other green vegetables, liver and eggs.

ESSENTIAL FATTY ACID INFORMATION
Omega-3 Fatty Acid Sources and Dosage Information:
DHA 500mg/day
EPA 500 mg/day
Alpha Linolenic Acid 1,000mg/day

Fatty acid synthesis involves the creation of fatty acids from the body's own blood sugar. Lipogenesis (fat creation) and glycolysis (glucose breakdown) are the key processes behind fatty acid synthesis which is modified by the acetyl-Coenzyme A (acetyl-CoA). Synthesis occurs mostly in the liver, but also within lactating mammary glands and fat tissue. Most acetyl-CoA is formed in the mitochondria.

ESSENTIAL FATTY ACID BIOCHEMISTRY			
Omega-3 Fatty Acid Pathway		*Omega-6 Fatty Acid Pathway*	
Alpha-Linoleic Acid (ALA)		*Linoleic Acid (LA)*	
↓		↓	
Steridonic Acid		*Gamma-linolenic Acid (GLA)*	
↓		↓	
Eicosatraenoic Acid		*Dihomo Gamma-linolenic Acid (DGLA)*	
↓		↓	
Eicosapentaenoic Acid (EPA)	*⇔Decosahexaic Acid (DHA)*	*Arachidonic Acid (AA)*	*Membrane Phospholipids*
↓	↓	↓	
PGE3	*LTB5*	*PGE2*	*LTB4*
Anti-inflammatory prostaglandins (3-series)	*Anti-inflammatory leukotrienes (5-series)*	*Inflammatory prostaglandins (2-series)*	*Inflammatory leukotrienes (4-series)*

Omega-3 and omega-6 fatty acids are polyunsaturated fatty acids that are required nutrients. Essential fatty acids are chains of carbon and hydrogen with a carboxylic end. They are required for the body's chemical pathways, yet cannot be manufactured by the body. Alpha-linolenic acid, eicosapentaenoic acid (EPA) and docosahexaenoic acid (DHA) are three are omega-3 acids required for humans and may be essential to the body's status regarding disease and development.

Omega-3 and omega-6 fatty acids are essential to good health. It has been theorized that our bodies would benefit greatly by eating a one-to-one ratio of omega-3 and omega-6 due to the fact that they tend to have equal yet opposite effects upon the human body. The average American consumes several times the necessary dosage of omega-6 fatty acids daily.

Food sources for omega-3 and omega-6 fatty acids are fish, shellfish, flaxseed, hemp seed, soya oil, canola oil, chia seeds, pumpkin seeds, sunflower seeds, leafy vegetables and walnuts. The body seems to more readily absorb fatty acids from animal sources rather than plant sources. Most American diets lack omega-3 and omega-6 fatty acids, and balancing of them may have tremendous health benefits. It is recommended that fish and shellfish be eaten three times per week.

Essential fatty acids serve multiple functions in the body. They affect inflammation, mood, cellular signaling and behavior. Omega-3 fatty acids are important for metabolic pathways required to break down large fatty acids. Depending upon the circumstance, they also promote or inhibit DNA replication. Essential fatty acids also affect the lifespan of cardiac cells. Lack of essential fatty acids or an imbalance of them may cause disease, including osteoporosis and skin disease. High omega-3 fatty acids are linked to decreased rates of depression and create other chemicals critical for synaptic transmission and brain and spinal fluids.

Recent statistics indicate that nearly 99% of people in the United States do not eat enough omega 3 fatty acids (Whole Foods, 2014). Unfortunately, the symptoms of omega-3 fatty acid deficiency are not easy to determine, but include lack of energy, skin irritation, poor hair and nail condition, constipation, frequent colds, depression, lack of focus, tiredness, and joint pain.

MINERAL INFORMATION

Absorption of Minerals

The ionic form of minerals is important for mineral absorbability. Colloidal minerals from humic shale extracts predominantly contain sulfates of iron and aluminum and traces of metal hydroxides. Many of the minerals in humic shale extracts are present in ionic forms. This may make it easier for them to cross cellular membranes. Mineral bioavailability is facilitated by the way in which metals cross the intestinal mucosa. A variety of conditions may affect metal transport across the intestinal mucosa. These factors can act at the brush border membrane, within the cytosol, and at the basolateral membrane. Metal ions, probably bound to intracellular ligands, cross the cytosol and are extruded across the basolateral membrane into the portal circulation. Once a metal ion enters the enterocyte, it may be used by the cell for its own metabolic needs or released in the circulation for the metabolic needs of other tissues. The liquid supplements usually are acidic; specifically, they are formulated to contain citric acid, ascorbic acid, and other substances that increase the bioavailability of minerals such as carbohydrates (glucose, lactose), polyols (sorbitol), amino acids (arginine, lysine), vegetable gums, peptides, and emulsifying agents. Solid vitamin-mineral preparations instead contain inert excipients and are usually buffered so as not to cause gastric discomfort on ingestion, although this may reduce mineral bioavailability. The bioavailability of a mineral in the body is governed by multiple factors, including body stores, hormonal regulation, the chemical form of the nutrient, and concomitant nutrient intake.

When glucose is used in used for calcium administration, net calcium absorption increased by fourfold.

Typical Mineral Absorption and Optimizing Factors

Mineral	Absorption	Optimizing factors
Calcium	25–35%	Vitamin D
Magnesium	21–27%	Vitamin D
Iron (non-heme)	5–10%	Vitamin C, ligand binder
Zinc	33–41%	Ligand binder
Copper	30–50%	Ligand binder
Selenium	50–80%	Incorporation into selenomethionine
Chromium	0.4–2.5%	Vitamin C, ligand binder
Manganese	1–3.5%	unknown

Absorbability = Bioavailability
While the ultimate absorption of minerals by the human body is dependent upon numerous factors including homeostasis, body stores, and hormonal regulation, the absorbability of minerals (their availability for absorption) is also affected by the form in which the minerals are ingested. The solubility of a mineral has been shown to enhance its bioavailability. Thus, there is scientific evidence that colloidal minerals may be more efficient, a preferred vehicle for absorption, than minerals in solid forms.

There is evidence that mineral deficiencies contribute to disease. For example, iron deficiency is a frequent finding in Rheumatoid Arthritis. Deficiencies of other minerals, such as potassium and magnesium, and possibly zinc and chromium, may predispose a person to carbohydrate intolerance. Intakes of selenium above RDA have been shown to have an anticancer effect in humans. Zinc deficiency has been linked to anorexia. Calcium and magnesium supplementation has been shown to reduce blood pressure in clinical studies.

There is evidence that the nutritional need for mineral intake is not being met, especially in certain subpopulations. Supplementation with minerals is recommended to complement dietary intake and avoid deficiencies. Mineral supplements are associated with different absorptive capacities.

Mineral absorption is affected by what we eat. Consuming fiber with vitamin and mineral supplements inhibits their absorption.

Some foods combined with salts reduce absorption. Phosphorus reduces calcium absorption. Protein-rich foods also contain phosphorus, which reduces calcium absorption.

However, owing to toxicity, immunogenicity, and lack of specificity, these delivery methods are being replaced by specific viral machinery that lacks pathogenic components (Rajendran et al., 2010).

Although the body's absorption of minerals depends in large part on their solubility, we must be very careful not to equate solubility of the salt containing a mineral with absorption of that mineral (Casiday and Frey, 2013).

Combined Mineral Administration Effects

If we consume too much calcium, and without sufficient magnesium, the excess calcium is not utilized correctly and may actually become toxic, causing painful conditions in the body. Many researchers and nutritionists now believe magnesium is more important than calcium in order to maintain healthy bones. In addition, magnesium is responsible for more than three hundred biochemical reactions, all necessary for optimum health. Magnesium plays a vital role in digestion, energy production, muscle contraction and relaxation, bone formation, and cell division. In addition, magnesium is a key nutrient in the proper functioning of the heart, the kidneys, the adrenals, and the entire nervous system. Magnesium, copper, iron, and calcium can all compete for absorption; therefore too much of one can lower blood levels of the others.

Diabetes

Deficiencies of certain minerals, such as potassium and magnesium and possibly zinc and chromium, may predispose a person to carbohydrate intolerance. More than 30 percent of ambulatory diabetic patients without renal insufficiency are magnesium deficient on a multifactorial basis according to one study. Some studies in older subjects with diabetes have suggested some benefit from zinc supplementation in healing skin ulcerations.

CALCIUM
RDA for Calcium is 1000mg with an upper limit of 2500mg per day. Calcium (Ca) is available in milk products, tofu, salmon, sardines, green leafy vegetables (not spinach or Swiss chard) and fortified products. Too much calcium may increase prostate cancer risk. Calcium may reduce the risk for colonic tumors as has been suggested in a number of studies. A nineteen-year study in Chicago demonstrated a 50-percent reduction in colon cancer risk in men with a daily intake of 3.75µg vitamin D and 75-percent reduction in men with a daily intake above 1200mg calcium. A similar study on women in Iowa further supported the hypothesis that vitamin D and/or calcium protect against colon cancer. Calcium helps build bones and teeth, aids in muscle movements, nerve transmission, hormone secretion, blood pressure control and blood clotting. Vitamin D3 is a necessary co-factor for calcium deposition.

CHLORIDE
RDA for chloride 750mg daily and is commonly measured as part of sodium chloride (salt) intake. Chloride (Cl) is part of the osmoregulation of all body fluids and a component of stomach acid in the form of HCl (hydrogen chloride) which aids digestion.

CHROMIUM (Cr)
RDA is 35mcg for men and 25 mcg for women and found in yeast, nuts, cheese, meat, fish and poultry. It is part of the glucose metabolic pathway and modulates the activity of insulin in maitenance of glucose levels in the blood.

COPPER
Copper inhibits Vitamin C absorption and has an RDA of 900mcg with an upper limit of 10,000mcg being easily absorbed from foods such as shellfish, liver, nuts, whole grain, prunes and beans. Copper (Cu) is part of blood cell development and iron metabolism.

FLUORIDE
RDA is 4mg for men and 3mg for women with an upper limit of 10mg daily which has been found to be harmful to children. It is found in fluoridated water, toothpaste, some teas and seafood. Fluoride (Fl) protects teeth from cavities and supports bone development.

IODINE
RDA is 150mcg with an upper limit of 1100mcg and is found in seafood, processed food, and iodized salt. Iodine (I) is an essential component of thyroid actions that affects nerve and muscle functions, body metabolism and growth. If you have temperature regulation issues and/or goiter conditions, Iodine deficiency may be the problem.

IRON
Iron provides the ability for the red blood cells and muscles to gather oxygen and gives blood its red color, deficiency (anemia) due to poor dietary intake or gastrointestinal blood loss. Anemia is a frequent finding in patients with chronic inflammatory rheumatic diseases. Selenium may increase anemia. Iron (Fe) is involved in many metabolic pathways including protein production for hormones, collagen and neurotransmitters. RDA is 8mg for men and 18mg for women and is found in vegetables and fortified grain products.

MAGNESIUM (Mg)
Magnesium deficiency has been shown to induce anorexia (uncommon weight loss) in rats. RDA for Magnesium is 420mg for men and 320mg for women and is commonly available in green vegetables, nuts, beans, whole-wheat products and milk. Magnesium along with calcium plays a role in muscle activity, blood clotting, blood pressure control and bone development.

Magnesium and Memory
In a study published January 28, 2010, in *Neuron*, neuroscientists from the Massachusetts Institute of Technology (MIT) and Tsinghua University in Beijing found that increasing brain magnesium improves learning abilities, working memory, and short- and long-term memory in rats. The magnesium also helped older rats perform better on a battery of learning tests. Because magnesium is an essential ion for normal cellular functions and body health, many physiological functions are impaired with the reduction of body magnesium. The researchers cite that only 32 percent of Americans get the recommended daily allowance of magnesium (Broder, 2013).

Magnesium and Hypertension
In epidemiological studies in which high blood pressure was correlated with dietary food records, higher magnesium intake was associated with decreased diastolic pressure. With adult women in another study, dietary magnesium (and calcium) was independently inversely related to hypertension. Hypertensive patients on thiazide diuretics given magnesium supplements showed a related effect drop in blood pressure.

MANGANESE
Manganese RDA is 2.3mg for men and 1.8mg for women with an upper limit of 11mg and is found in nuts, beans, whole grains, and tea, helps in the process of forming bones. It aids bone development, and is involved with metabolism of amino acids, cholesterols, and carbohydrates. If taken in excess, manganese (Mn) can cause liver damage.

MOLYBDENUM
RDA is 45mcg with an upper limit of 2000mcg and is found in beans, nuts, grain and milk products. Molybdenum (Mb) is involved in several enzyme biochemical pathways.

PHOSPHORUS
RDA is 700mg with and upper limit of 4000mg daily. Many foods such as milk products, poultry, meat, fish, liver, peas, almonds, potatoes and broccoli contain phosphorus (P). It is part of the bone development process, DNA synthesis, food conversion into energy and the phospho- part of many metabolic pathways of the body. Deficiency in phosphorus may cause weakness, pain, and bone ailments.

POTASSIUM
RDA for potassium (K+) is 2000mg and is found in milk, meat, fruits, beans, vegetables and grain. Potassium is responsible for much of the body's metabolism including nerve conduction, muscle actions, body fluid homeostasis, blood pressure regulation and bone development.

SELENIUM
RDA is 55mcg with an upper limit of 400mcg daily. Selenium (Se) is found in seafood, organ meats and walnuts and is an antioxidant that can neutralize free radicals. Selenium absorption is a key issue as a supplement. When examining the quality of life a significant ($p < 0.01$) improvement in arm movements and health feeling was evidenced in selenium-treated patients. Epidemiological evidence is also emerging for the beneficial effects of selenium supplementation in hypertension. Researchers have demonstrated that Selenium has an antihypertensive effect on spontaneously hypertensive rats.

Selenium Supplementation to Prevent Cancer
Selenium has been studied as an anti-carcinogenic agent for more than twenty-five years. These studies found that selenium in combination with other nutrients, particularly vitamins A and E, had an inhibitory effect on esophageal and stomach cancers. In a study of micronutrient supplementation, including selenium, on tobacco chewers and smokers in India developed fewer oral lesions than in the placebo group.

SODIUM (Na)
RDA for sodium (salt) 500mg, however an upper limit is not known some studies show average American sodium intake may be as high as 5000mg per day. Salt is found in many foods and occurs naturally in every living thing! Sodium is involved in all metabolic activities and indeed all cellular functions.

SULFUR (Su)
RDA for sulfur is unknown. Sulfur is a part of many amino acids and is therefore part of many proteins and functions as a molecular bridge in protein structures. Sulfur is found in all protein rich foods such as meats, poultry, milk, nuts and beans.

ZINC
RDA for Zinc (Zn) is 11mg for men and 8mg for women with an upper limit of 40mg and is commonly found in shellfish, red meat, poultry fortified foods, nuts and beans. Zinc has been indicated in improving immunity, wound healing, protein synthesis, and in the process of taste/smell senses.

Zinc and Brain and Other Disorders
There is evidence that zinc deficiency is associated with anorexia (eating disorder). Zinc deficiency has been shown to adversely affect brain growth, learning, and activity. In athletes, zinc deficiency can lead to anorexia, a significant loss in body weight, latent fatigue with decreased endurance, and a risk of osteoporosis.

VITAMIN AND MINERAL FORMULATIONS
This chapter shows the necessity of vitamins and minerals for normal metabolism. By definition these vitamins are necessary chemical components of essential

processes of life and are not easily available to sufficiency through average eating behavior. It is therefore incumbent upon the average person to supplement their diet with vitamins and minerals to provide for the normal biochemical maintenance of their body. Without vitamin and mineral enrichment to most peoples' diets there is a downhill pathway to some deficiency that will lead to a disease state down the line. Recent studies have shown that the people taking vitamins and especially high dose vitamins meant to improve the quality of peoples' lives are not getting the benefits of the administered supplements. When we look at the cellular actions necessary to have uptake of the vitamins and mineral presented which occurs mostly at the end of the digestive cycle we see that there is a chemical imbalance from the products taken compared to the cell membranes ability to transpose these molecules necessary to nutrition and metabolism from outside the cell to inside the cell. The next diagram shows that just placing a molecule in solution without an adequate delivery agent has no effect upon the metabolism of the animal. In this case, growth hormone (bST) is applied in solution with and without a delivery modifier, GroFish. With GroFish there is significant subsequent growth of the fish treated, however when the growth hormone, which is a large protein molecule, is applied in a solution without GroFish there is actually an inhibitory effect of the growth of the fish as compared to the untreated control fish. This research clearly shows that the presence of a substance in solution without adequate delivery mechanisms for the molecule to be absorbed by the cell can result in no effect to even a negative effect. Recent human studies for vitamin and mineral supplementation shows a similar result indicating that there needs to be an improvement of the delivery system for vitamins and minerals which by definition are necessary for normal metabolism.

Growth of Hybrid Striped Bass at Six Weeks with Various bST Applications

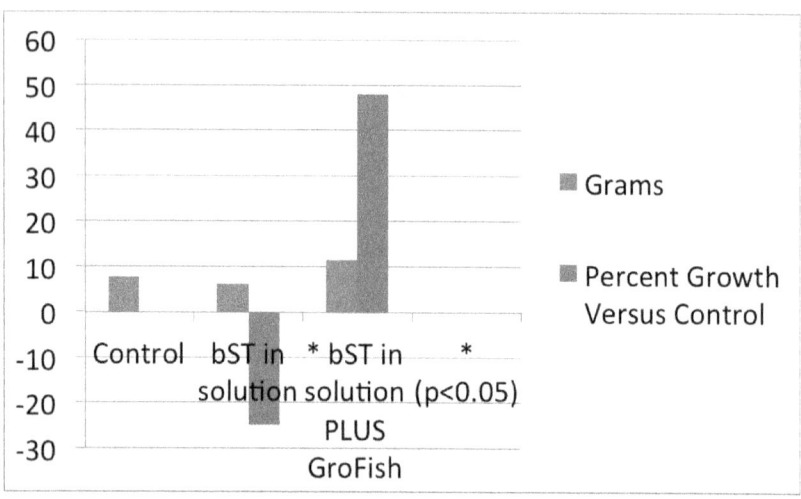

This graph shows the percentage of growth of hybrid striped bass that were treated with bST alone or GroFish™ and bST together. bST is a common growth hormone. Results show that bST and GroFish™ used together had an increase in growth by 48 percent, proving the effectiveness of GroFish's ability to get the bST absorption into the cells. Conveying bST without salt had no effect on growth, showing a suboptimal absorption of bST without salt in solution.

Recent Discovery:

BOOSTER™

- **Delivery enhancement process for pharmaceuticals, nutraceuticals, and cosmetic products using a patent-pending organic and food-safe technology.**

After reviewing thousands of medical, nutraceutical, and cosmetic formulas in the USP Dietary Supplements Compendium 2009–2010, it was found that almost none of these had an ionic formulation that, when presented to the cell wall, would be easily recognized for transfer or absorption into or past the cell wall. Therefore, successful absorption would require active transport, or otherwise only a limited amount of the desired product or active ingredient would be absorbed. Immediately, it became clear that there needed to be a better way to present active ingredients for delivery into the cell.

Chapter 9. Adopting New Patterns for Cosmetics

Women apply retinol, vitamin B_{12}, collagen, and other large-molecule products regularly to their skin. However, the normal skin cell absorbs very little to none of these elements. With the understanding for new mechanisms of cell metabolism and use of BOOSTER™, which opens up the cell pores for large-molecule entries; the benefits for cosmetic product use can be immense.

The face and body have been a palette for decorating, adornment, and beauty modification and as an activity that is among the oldest, most widespread, and persistent of human behaviors. The practice has continued since reinforcement of "how do I look?" occurs in all societies that decorate the face and body. Cosmetics and other decorations of the body are widespread and persistent because they are a part of what defines us as individuals and as humans. Cosmetics help to give us our identity (Russell, 2013).

The beauty-care products industry is composed of establishments primarily engaged in manufacturing beauty products externally applied to enhance the beauty of skin, hair, nails, lips, and eyes. Increased demand for multi-feature products such as moisturizing cream with sun protection and anti-aging or anti-wrinkle properties are likely to drive market growth (Market Research Reports, 2013).

According to the latest market research reports, the global beauty care industry will hit $265 billion by 2017global beauty care industry will hit $265 billion by 2017 (Market Research Reports, 2013).

The global cosmetics industry is broken down into six main categories, skincare being the largest one out of them all, accounting for 33.8 percent of the global market in 2012 (Schulz, 2013).

The United States is the biggest cosmetic market in the world, with estimated total revenue of about 54.89 billion US dollars and employing about 53,619 people in 2012 (Schulz, 2013).

Cosmetic sales are estimated to continue to grow in both the United States and other global markets, as many consumers feel that beauty products help in achieving social and economic goals (Schulz, 2013).

Research

Beginning May 21, 2012, human trials for two popular skin care products—Deep Moist Milk Chamomile (125 mL) and Deep Moist Skin Toner Chamomile (125 mL)—were assessed using human subjects. Both products appeared to be consistent with their description and of extremely high quality compared to other "high-end" consumer products currently available in the US cosmetics market.

The intent was to utilize the Innovative Drug Manufacturing LLC product BOOSTER™ to improve skin moisturization as well as to improve skin tone. After several weeks of trials, the improved products were noted to give an "additional moisturizing effect as well as a skin-tightening result." Over several days, it was noticed that "sagging under the eyes" was significantly reduced, skin tone and tightness was greatly improved, and skin was significantly moisturized compared to the non-treated products.

Overall, the application seemed to have the effect of lasting several days and, after several days, the test participants noticed lasting effects they had never seen before. Obviously, BOOSTER™ was transferring the compound's active ingredients more efficiently into the cells, which in turn gave a more lasting effect. Several additional trials have seen similar results with skin-care products including facial masques, facial cleansers, sunblock lotion, hand cream, facial pad cleansers, and more.

Topical Action

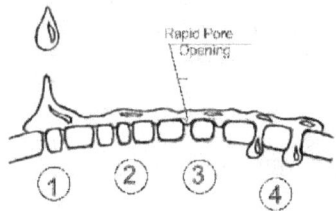

This diagram shows the process of topical application of a BOOSTER™ product with the active ingredient applied to skin. At step 1, the product is applied. During step 2, the pores start to open. In step 3, the skin's pores open, allowing the active ingredient to be absorbed. In step 4, the active ingredient has permeated into the skin and will achieve its function.

Chapter 10. Advances in Chemotherapy

Chemotherapy has advanced significantly in the past fifty years, from very few effective agents being available to numerous drug agents being available today. Unfortunately, the majority of chemotherapy agents have significant side effects that also affect the overall well-being of the patient.

Innovative Drug Manufacturing LLC has recently applied for a patent (Methods and Compositions for Enhancing the Uptake of an Active Ingredient) for a new trademarked product named BOOSTER™. In a related study conducted by GVK Biosciences Pvt. Ltd., mice treated with BOOSTER™ using a high-level dose of vitamin D_3 had a greatly increased uptake of vitamin D_3 compared to the control. The conclusion of the study was:

> *The pooled urine concentration of vitamin D_3 is more in the enhanced feed group (group-3) than in the control feed group (group-2), 9.8 times the vitamin D_3 dosed controls and 31.8 times the vitamin D_3 untreated controls during feeding time. Therefore, the application of **BOOSTER™** very significantly increased the absorption of vitamin D_3 in this mammalian model.*

Similar human studies with cosmetic products and topical analgesic uses have shown success in improved uptake and advancing results from these applications.

Recently, an application of an erlotinib-based chemotherapeutic drug was evaluated. This drug, which causes several side effects, is likely a candidate for BOOSTER™ treatment. This application would allow for a decreased amount of the drug erlotinib being applied with BOOSTER™ at a reduced dosage to achieve standard results with much fewer side effects. Other drugs that may benefit from BOOSTER™ formulations include capecitabine, cyclophosphamide, etoposide, idarubicin, vinorelbine, and imatinib. We encourage drug manufacturers and other interested parties to contact us to advance the BOOSTER™ applications for chemotherapeutic use.

A Purdue University researcher demonstrated the details of how drugs are released within a cancer cell. By improving the ability to deliver drugs to a specific target without affecting surrounding cells will benefit cancer therapies. Linking vitamins, toxic chemotherapeutic drugs are transported directly to the cancer cell and do not harm healthy cells (Purdue University, 2006).

With small molecules, unique delivery mechanisms can provide improvement in delivery efficiency, which in turn allows significant decreases in administered doses of active ingredients over traditional formulations, resulting in improved benefit/risk ratios for active ingredients with that normally have poor therapeutic windows.

As discussed in previous chapters, utilizing water soluble active ingredients with an efficient delivery system can allow soluble active ingredients across the blood-brain barrier, which has been previously a highly efficient barrier to many classes of active ingredients.

Lipid modifications could cause the drugs to be non-specifically adsorbed onto the membranes at the injection site and therefore reduce the bioavailability of the compound. Several anticancer drugs have been targeted to endosomes by conjugating drugs to ligands that are internalized to endosomes through receptor-mediated interactions. Ligands such as transferrin, folate and low-density lipoproteins have been exploited for drug targeting, as these ligands show high affinity for their cognate receptors. As these receptors are often overexpressed in malignant tumors, conjugation of drugs or dyes to the ligands of these receptors aids specific tumor targeting for therapy or imaging. However, the level of overexpression that is required to see differences between the tumor and normal tissue remains unclear. Iron loaded transferrin binds to the transferrin receptor (TFR)—a transmembrane protein that is present in almost all cells—and is sorted to early endosomes, in which the ligand is released from its receptor. Release enables the delivery of transferrin (or transferrin conjugated drugs) to the early endosomal lumen and sorting of the receptor to recycling compartments. Antitumor drugs such as doxorubicin and cisplatin have been coupled to transferrin and showed more cytotoxic potency than unconjugated drugs (Rajendran et al., 2010).

The folate receptor is also of interest for cancer therapy as it is upregulated in many epithelial cancers. Folate has high receptor affinity, which enables efficient binding of folate conjugates to the receptors. Folate receptor targeted delivery of liposomal doxorubicin to folate receptor expressing cells increased the cellular uptake and cytotoxicity of doxorubicin. Polyethylene glycol–folate conjugates of thioctic acid carrying gold nanoparticles were used against ovarian cancer cells and were also efficiently targeted to the endosomal compartment. Other ligands such as vitamin B12 and low density lipoprotein like nanoparticles have also been used successfully as drug conjugates. (Rajendran et al., 2010)

Summary

By utilizing BOOSTER™ technology, chemotherapeutic drugs can be even more effective at the cellular level. Increased cellular penetration provides significant decreases in administration doses. Using a more effective delivery technology would allow for reducing the actual dose and could decrease the side effects of chemotherapy.

Chapter 11. Other Uses for Enhanced Delivery

Enhanced delivery not only speeds up delivery of vitamins, nutrition, or pharmaceutical products, but it increases the cellular nutrition support within the body, building stronger cells and increasing immunity.

- Transdermal and by-mouth delivery

  BOOSTER™ products can be taken in the body through the skin (transdermal) or by taking a pill by mouth. The most effective method depends upon the types of cells you are trying to affect. Transdermal delivery may be most effective with topical skin applications, such as Botox.

- Oral cancer chemotherapeutics

  Oral chemotherapy medicines are given by mouth in the form of capsules, tablets, or liquid. With BOOSTER™ enhancing the delivery of the active ingredient of a medicine, it would be unnecessary to use as much of the active ingredient, and it would also increase the effectiveness of chemotherapy. The intent would be to cure as many people of cancer as possible.

- Traditional medicine

  The World Health Organization defines traditional medicine as "a sum total of the knowledge, skills, and practices based on the theories, beliefs, and experiences indigenous to different cultures, whether explicable or not, used in the maintenance of health as well as in the prevention, diagnosis, improvement or treatment of physical and mental illness" (World Health Organization, 2013). In herbal medicines in which the active ingredient is known, the creation of these medicines could be standardized.

  Herbal medicines include herbs, herbal materials, herbal preparations, and finished herbal products that contain as active ingredients parts of plants, or other plant materials, or combinations (World Health Organization, 2013).

— Herbs include only plant materials such as leaves, flowers, fruit, seed, stems, bark, roots, etc.
— Herbal materials are herbs made into juices, gums, oils, and resins.
— Herbal preparations include powders, extracts, tinctures, and fatty oils of herbal materials.
— Finished herbal products are defined as being herbal preparations made from one or more herbs.
— A key benefit of BOOSTER™ for traditional medicine is that BOOSTER™ very significantly changes the delivery (Sonnenschein, 2012). A large, complex molecule necessitates the ability to use smaller quantities of the active ingredient for increased absorption. Many of these traditional medicines are based on expensive extracts to produce, and by utilizing BOOSTER™ the net effects will reduce cost to both the manufacturer and the consumer as well as increase the efficiency of the delivery of the active ingredient.

- Spray analgesics and other painkiller application

These are painkillers that are taken by spraying the medicine either on your body or in your mouth, typically underneath the tongue. Alternatively, a topical method can help pinpoint the part of the body in which you need relief from pain. With enhanced delivery with BOOSTER™, additional healing and pain relief may be achieved. Sublingual sprays can hasten the delivery of the drug within your body. Several human trials have shown improved time of delivery; increased pain reduction and increased duration of the analgesic effect with BOOSTER™ treated sprays, topical applications and oral tablet based utilization.

- Nanoparticles, drug carriers in the submicron size range, have been shown to enhance the therapeutic efficacy of encapsulated drugs by increasing and sustaining the delivery of the drug inside the cell. However, the use of nanoparticles for small molecular weight, water-soluble drugs has been limited by poor drug encapsulation efficiency and rapid release of the encapsulated drug (Chavanpatil et al., 2007). It may be worth considering the effect that BOOSTER™ may have on the delivery of the nanoparticles.

Chapter 12. Toxin Absorption

In 2011, the population of Japan became exposed to an extreme health hazard from the Fukushima Daiichi nuclear power plant. This radioactive exposure, which is based upon elementary metal isotopes, provided for an opportunity to design a process to absorb metal-based toxins within the body and from the skin. Metal elimination technology was developed for precisely this purpose.

Since 2011, the radiation has spread through the wind, but more importantly through the water in the Pacific Ocean. We now have a crisis of enormous proportion that has no regulation. As these radioactive particles are distributed through the water certain species will be consuming at the various food chain levels to where the highest-level predator will also be a storage mechanism for an untold amount of radiation. As we increase of our consumption of these species, we see more and more cases radiation poisoning developing from human consumption activity.

Residual Incremental Increase in Radiation

Researchers are concerned about the effects of the radioactive water on sea life and those who eat it. Last year, scientists reported that Pacific bluefin tuna migrating from coastal Japan to the waters off Southern California contained radioactive cesium isotopes from the Fukushima plant. The safety of Pacific fish following the disaster is up for debate (Light and Kamp, 2013).

Because ocean currents disperse radiation far and wide via giant eddies and whirlpools, the full impact on our ocean food supply may not be known for years (Poland, 2013).

Even low levels of toxins can have a significant effect upon the human body, including fetuses. An increasing number of clinicians and scientists are becoming convinced that these chemical exposures contribute to obesity, endometriosis, diabetes, autism, allergies, cancer, and other diseases (Hunt, 2013).

With radioactive toxins going into the food chain, there was a defined need to develop an oral pill that could be safely administered in the morning and in the evening to allow for significant absorption of potential metal-based radioactive toxins internal to the digestive system. Additionally, a skin-applied sunblock with absorptive capacity would be tested for surface or airborne metal based toxin removal.

Research Results of Metal Elimination Technology

Pill Results

At fifteen minutes from original application, the first natural product alone yielded a 98-percent reduction (0.01 mg/L iron). Also at fifteen minutes after application, the organic antioxidant in combination with another natural product yielded a 100-percent reduction (0.00 mg/L iron). Both products remained successful at thirty minutes after application as well.

Sunblock Testing

The testing showed a material with a SPF40 sunblock capacity containing titanium dioxide which is less injurious to the skin and included a series of moisturizers that left the skin softer as well as the general lotion was lighter in texture than traditional sunblock. Absorption using Sequestar Iron 6% added to one liter of water and reduce solution through titration to 0.5 mg/L using NutraFin Test for Iron (0.0–1.0 mg/L) made by Hagen showed that an iron solution 0.5 mg/L after thirty minutes from application of new sunblock using 10 mL of the iron solution yielded 0.00 mg/L iron in solution (100 percent removal). Therefore, this achieved the goal, including a capacity to very significantly reduce ($p<0.001$) potential metal and other toxic materials on the skin.

Results

There was a fivefold reduction in iron from the sunblock application compared to the control. This report shows that the application can reduce metals and toxins up to 100 percent within thirty minutes of application upon the skin while improving skin care.

Chapter 13. Topical Botox

For centuries, the fountain of youth has been sought by explorers in the hope of never experiencing natural death or aging. Today, plastic surgery is a common vehicle for achieving a youthful appearance on the visage. One less invasive technique utilized by plastic surgeons is called Botox. Botox is a prescription medicine that is injected into the area around the side of the eyes to improve the look of moderate to severe crow's feet wrinkles in adults for a short period of time (temporary) (Wikipedia).

Botox® is administered by a health-care professionals as a simple, nonsurgical treatment that is injected directly into the muscles and works by affecting muscle movement.

Approximately 11.8 million Botox cosmetic procedures have been administered in the United States since 2002 (Wikipedia).

Based on the ability for BOOSTER™ technology to move large molecules into the cell without injection Botox applications could be made much safer and easier to use. Botox could be reformulated into a topical cream and produce the same results as if it were injected. This could use less toxin due to the preferential delivery system that BOOSTER™ provides.

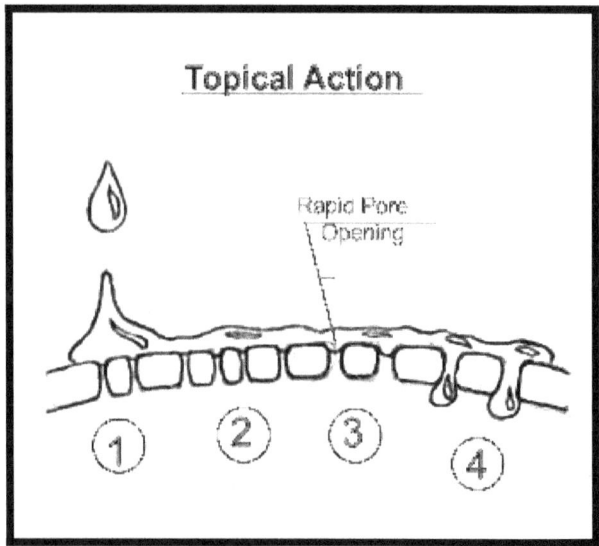

This diagram shows the process of topical application of a BOOSTER™ product with the active ingredient applied to skin. At step 1, the product is applied. During step 2, the pores start to open. In step 3, the skin's pores open, allowing the active ingredient to be absorbed. In step 4, the active ingredient has permeated into the skin and will achieve its function.

Chapter 14. New Frontiers

Gene Therapy
The GroFish™ patent provides a mechanism for large molecular intercellular delivery without an injection. Current genetic technology is allowing for new proteins that are developed based upon particular DNA characteristics of the patient. However, this gene therapy has a protein molecule that works in an in vitro (in the laboratory) basis. It needs to be provided intracellularly in order for it to work in the patient. The GroFish™ process, using BOOSTER™ technology, can open up cell pores to allow the macromolecular-sized genetic material in and allow the health applications to work.

With BOOSTER™ technology, the health of an individual—down to the cellular level—can significantly improve every aspect of health, even extending lifespans. As cells become healthier, they are more able to resist diseases, thereby extending the length of life. As a whole, BOOSTER™ treated products can improve the quality of life through holistic health.

Delivery Using Nanoparticles
Nanoparticles are microscopically dispersed-phase particles that are used as alternative delivery devices to liposomes or viral vectors. Nanomedicine, as a new field has shown promise in the delivery of drugs. The nanoparticles encapsulate in the particulate matter to be administered. These nanoparticles can enhance stability and the drug-dissolution rate. Encapsulating with appropriate uptake mechanics might enable specific cellular uptake and specific targeting to subcellular areas. Whereas by traditional methods the smaller particulates could be taken up by fluid-phase endocytosis, the larger ones might be phagocytosed , the use of BOOSTER™ may allow for additional clarity of use in these nano-applications including subcellular delivery of nanoparticles released into the cytosol. (Rajendran, 2010).

Chapter 15. Agricultural Applications

The application of BOOSTER™ technology is not only for animal cells. It has significant success in plant life as well. Applying the BOOSTER™ technology to seeds has been found to increase the plant's growth and may decrease its susceptibility to disease. Since the BOOSTER™ technology increases growth, it is theorized that the uptake of nutrients within the plant is also increased. Moreover, the addition of iron and/or sulfur to fertilizer can purify nitrogenous effluents and therefore decrease runoff pollution, which causes hypoxic zones, also known as "dead zones." A desired chemical state can be achieved by aiding natural processes in creating elemental nitrogen and oxygen at the end of the ammonia cycle using the following equation:

$NH_3(aq) + H_2O(l) \Leftrightarrow NH_4^+(aq) + OH(aq)$

$N_{2(g)} + O_{2(g)} ==> 2NO_{(g)}$, then
then $2NO_{(g)} + O_{2(g)} ==> 2NO_{2(g)}$

Through the process of eutrophication from our nation's inland crop production, runoff that contains elevated amounts of nutrients from different fertilizers used on farmlands has caused excessive marine plant growth, specifically in the Gulf of Mexico through the Mississippi River, forming what has come to be known as a "dead zone," or a hypoxic water zone, which has grown inhabitable to marine life. Through the experiment with variables of H_2O and H_2O + bacteria and subvariables including fertilizer, fertilizer + sulfur, fertilizer + iron, fertilizer + sulfur + iron, iron, sulfur, and iron + sulfur in the vessels in which corn has grown, measurements of the resulting pH, ammonia, nitrate, nitrite, and phosphorous content of the runoff water were recorded, analyzed, and observed.

Here are the results of this research project:

Corn Data Averages and Tables

COMPARISON				
	Nitrite	Nitrate	Ammonia	Phosphorus
Fertilizer – H_2O	0.7	20.8	4.2	2.0
Iron – H_2O	0.9	8.3	1.6	1.5
Fertilizer + Sulfur + Iron - H_2O	0.3	8.3	4.5	1.2

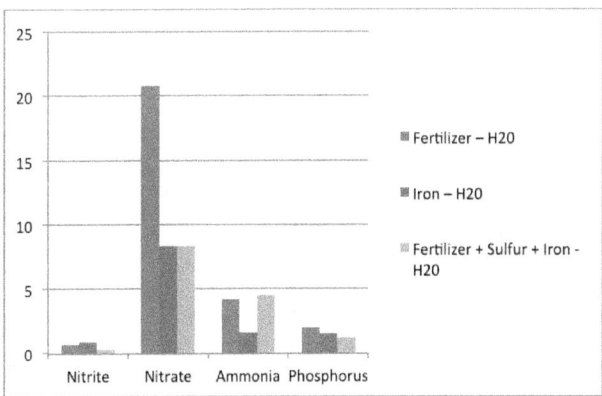

Chemicals measured were nitrite, nitrate, ammonia, and phosphorus.

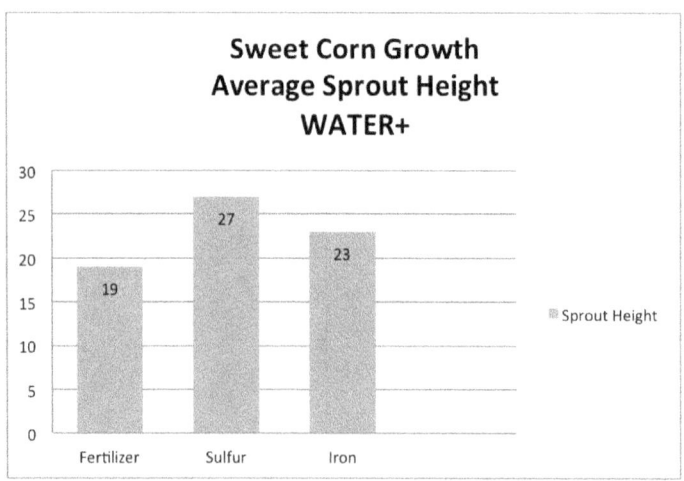

Sulfur provides a nutrient for the reduction of nitrate (NO_3), which is known for creating the dead zone. When adequate time is allowed for sulfur to dissolve within the ecosystem, the chemical reactions resulting from the sulfur introductions proceed in a balanced and predictable manner such that sulfur oxidizes to sulfate ion, and the nitrate is reduced to nitrogen, in both dissolved and gaseous forms. Low nitrate levels *in situ* and *ex situ* promote overall well-being for flora and fauna. The effects on fauna include improved growth rate, resistance to disease, improved breeding behavior, and decreased dead-zone prevalence.

These statistics indicate that the addition of sulfur and iron can aid in the decrease of nitrite, ammonia, and nitrate in addition to increasing the growth of corn significantly compared the fertilizer-only control. Much more research needs to be done on a longer-term basis and eventually field trials including looking at crop yield and seed analysis for comparative nutritional concentrations.

In 1995, the World Aquarium started adding sulfur doses to our ten-thousand-gallon shark tank. This graph shows the progressive measurements of nitrates.

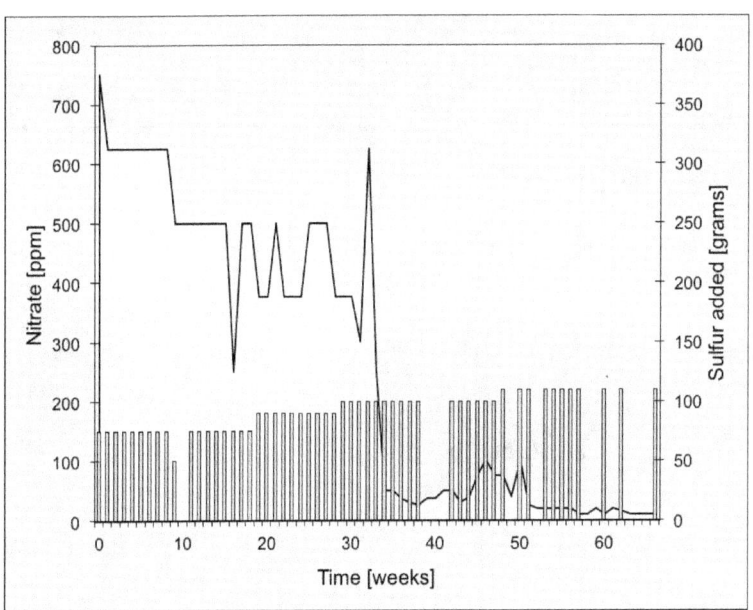

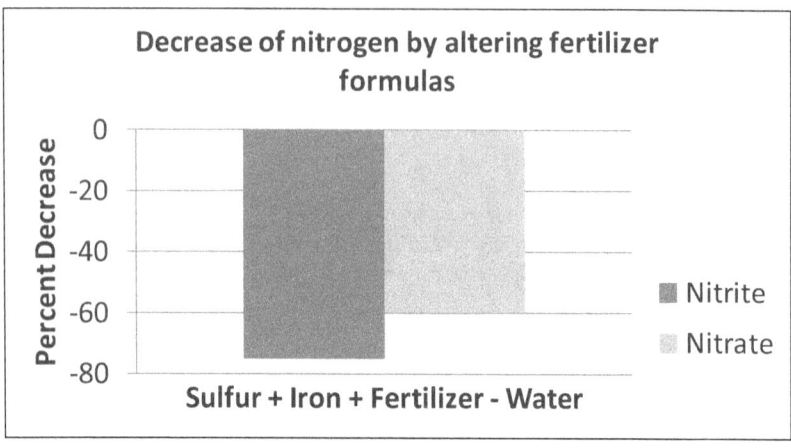

Fertilizer Effluent Effects

The addition of iron and/or sulfur to fertilizer can purify nitrogenous effluents and therefore decrease runoff pollution that causes hypoxic zones, also known as "dead zones."

In 2013, the World Aquarium tested the effects of granular and liquid fertilizers on aquatic ecosystems.

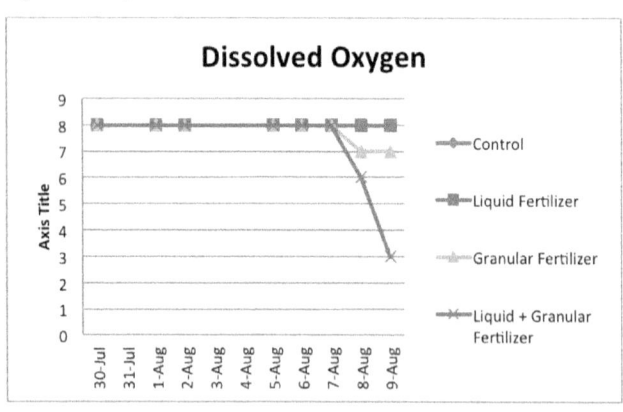

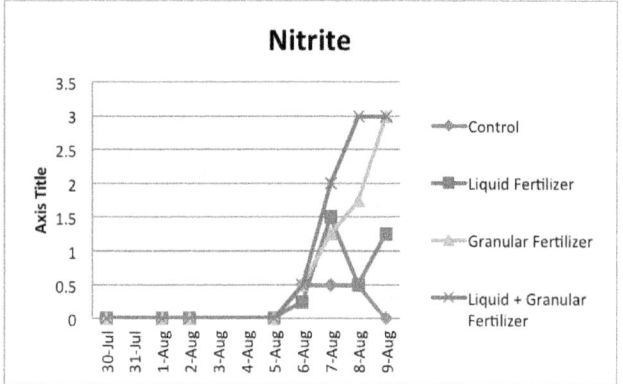

The mixture of granular and liquid fertilizers had the strongest results, with dissolved oxygen plummeting a total of five parts per million and nitrite levels raising three parts per million.

Livestock Feed
We are only at the beginning of understanding of the applications for agricultural uses for BOOSTER. Due to the complex nature of rumen function for cattle it may be possible to use BOOSTER technology in the animal feed to further improve uptake of nutrients as well as to stimulate health at the cellular level from feed additives. With recent changes regarding antibiotic use in the livestock industry, there is an increasing need to find organic solutions to improving health and productivity.

Chapter 16: GroFish™ Technology

What we place in farm fields and what we place in the aquaculture net pens all ends up running into our streams, rivers, and oceans. By looking more closely at the absorption of these nutrients and the nutrient effect upon living ecosystems, a reduction of pollution and an increase in ecosystem productivity can be achieved.

Aquaculture Effluent Effects

- Recent studies in mass aquaculture production show that farms can operate on a sustainable basis by utilizing improved feed formulation and filtration technology. Unfortunately, excess nitrogenous effluents can pollute surrounding waters in open ocean aquaculture net pens. Simple modifications can be made to significantly reduce effluents. Using GroFish™ technology in tandem with feed modification can reduce effluents.

GroFish™ Technology

One of the related applications of the BOOSTER™ technology is GroFish™. GroFish™ is a chemical-free, all-natural organic treatment to grow seafood healthier, larger, and faster. GroFish™ technology not only enhances the growth but also improves the resistance of treated animals against diseases. GroFish ™ satisfies the need for an environmentally friendly method to generate a more sustainable food source. Any creature living in water can be treated. So far, over thirty aquatic species treated include hybrid striped bass, carp, channel catfish, prawns, salmon, shrimp, abalone, trout, bullfrogs, tilapia, mussels, clams, sea cucumbers, and coral. Other aquatic species have been shown to increase growth, health, and feed conversion due to the fish treatment. GroFish™ Commercial research has been done in Chile on salmon; in China on shrimp, carp, sea cucumbers, grouper, and tilapia; in Norway on trout; in Sweden on trout; in Mexico on shrimp; in Vietnam on shrimp; in India on shrimp; in Panama on shrimp; and in the USA on prawn, shrimp, catfish, carp, bass, and trout.

Treatments are one-time and are beneficial to the further development of the cellular metabolism. Cells treated with this process tend to grow more mitochondria (the energy organelle of the cell), more Golgi bodies (the natural producer of hormones and other protective proteins), and more immunologically important cells (those that help with pathogen resistance). Animals treated with this patented technology tend to grow faster, be healthier, and live longer than the comparable nontreated control subjects.

How GroFish™ Works

The GroFish™ treatment is done by bathing aquatic species in a special saline solution, preferably when they are eyed-eggs or several days old for the best results. Treatment can be done for millions of organisms in only one day. After the treatment, nothing else has to be done, other than maintaining optimal water quality.

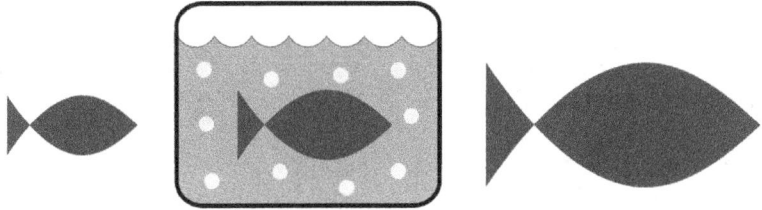

Aquaculture Process Improvement

The aquaculture process can becoming highly efficient in bringing aquatic species to market much faster and thereby increasing profits by utilizing the GroFish™ technology on these aquatic species. Also, feed modification can speed up the growth process while reducing expenditures. A great benefit of the GroFish™ treatment and feed modification being used simultaneously is the reduction of effluent pollution, thereby improving the water quality within the aquaculture pens as well as in the surrounding environment.

GroFish™ has great benefits:

- Animals that are treated with GroFish™ experience additional growth of between 22 and 75 percent more when kept under optimal water quality conditions compared to the same species within the same time frame with no treatment (chapter 15). This means that aquaculture farmers will get a return on their investment a lot faster.

- Worldwide, aquaculture has experienced outbreaks of diseases due to rising global water temperatures and pollution. GroFish™-treated animals appear to have enhanced immunity to these diseases, including WSV, VHS, and EMS. These diseases kill everything, except for those aquatic species treated with GroFish™.

DRASTIC INCREASE IN SURVIVAL

GroFish™ and Bacterial Resistance
Effects of Bacterial Pathogens on *P. vannamei* (White Shrimp)

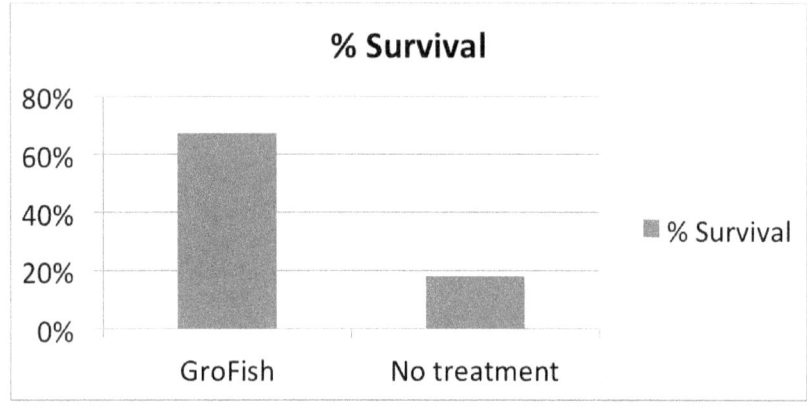

- Aquatic species such as salmon also experienced improved fatty acid content, such as omega-3 and other omega fatty acids, and increased glycogen content.

- When feed modification is used in tandem with the GroFish™ treatment, less protein is necessary for the feed, which costs less and maximizes profit. Increased feed efficiency = total reduction in feed costs. Also, feed modifications decrease the effluent effects downstream due to change in food formulation lessening the protein content, thereby decreasing the ammonia, resulting in a decrease of over 50 percent in downstream pollutants from aquaculture production facilities.

- GroFish™ can be used to treat virtually any creature living in water. It's not just for fish or even shellfish. It can be used to successfully treat sea cucumbers as well as corals.

- GroFish™-treated animals are easily feed-trained compared to animals that are not treated due to their ravenous appetite. Feed training reduces feed waste and the consequent effluent and pollution since the fish go to the water's surface due to the fact that they are hungrier, so less food is wasted, and species that were treated can be brought to market much faster.

- GroFish™ has been globally patented and protected by special process controls using specially treated organic products for a one-time treatment, in comparison to other aquaculture treatments needing augmentation or other continual provision in their grow-out portion.

- Best of all, up to twenty-five million aquatic animals can be treated in one day, which makes the GroFish™ process easy and efficient. There are no repeat treatments to deal with.

GroFish™ Results

Representative GroFish™ Results

Selected Species / Percentage of Size Increase Relative to Untreated Controls	
Shrimp	+58%
Salmon	+38%
Tilapia	+33%
Channel Catfish	+46%
Hybrid Striped Bass	+50%

Compared to the control group, 33 to 58 percent additional growth can be expected in shrimp, salmon, tilapia, channel catfish, and hybrid striped bass. Shrimp had the highest growth at 58 percent; tilapia had the lowest growth at 33 percent. When fish grow faster, they can be harvested sooner, bringing a profit to the aquaculture farmer.

REPRESENTATIVE RESULTS
Coho Salmon Smolt Growth Rate Graph

Twelve thousand Coho Salmon smolts (salmon that are approximately two months old) were given GroFish™ feed additive, GroFish™ treatment, GroFish™ treatment + feed additive, or nothing (control). The salmon treated with both GroFish™ and the feed additive had a 38 percent higher growth than the control group.

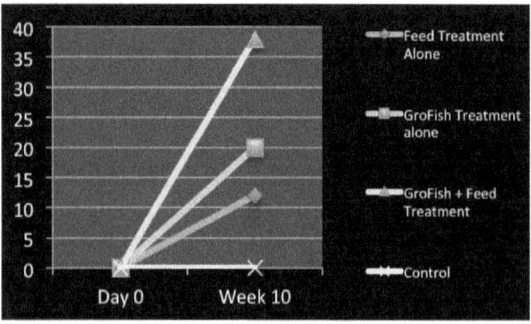

Percentage Size Larger Compared to Control	
	Week 10
Feed Treatment Alone	+12%
GroFish™ Treatment alone	+20%
GroFish™ + Feed Treatment	+38%
Control	+0%

Corals have also been tested using GroFish™ technology.

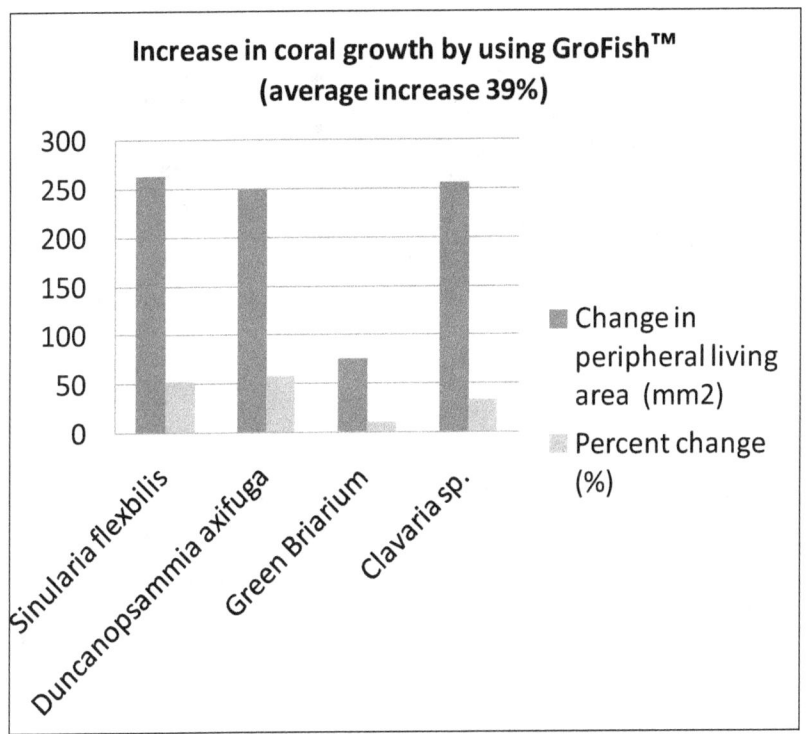

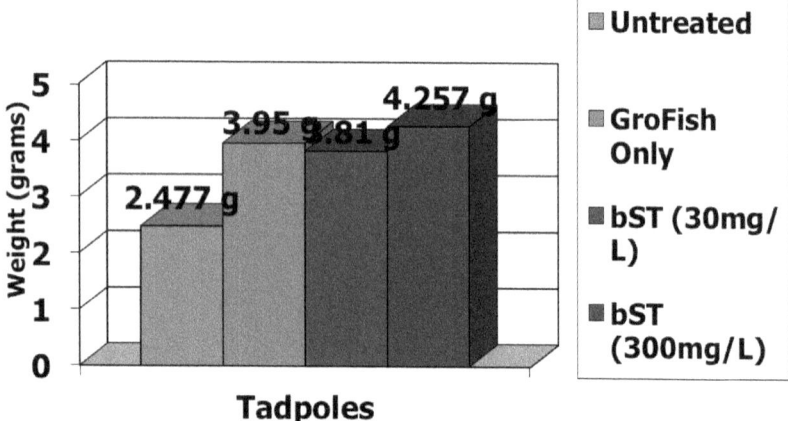

Demonstration of Endogenous Production of Growth Hormone by Comparison to Exogenous Application of bST

Bullfrog tadpoles were tested to see the effects of GroFish™ treatment versus bST in two different levels: 30mg/L and 300mg/L.

To make sure each experimental group was equitable, the following experimental conditions were enacted:

- All bullfrog tadpoles were fed the same type and amount of food per animal in each enclosure.
- The bullfrogs were kept in identically sized pens.
- All enclosures had identical filtration, temperature, and water quality.

Surprisingly, the GroFish™-treated tadpoles had almost as much growth as the tadpoles treated with 300mg/L of bST. The lower dose of bST (30mg/L) had 54 percent growth compared to the higher dose (300mg/L) at 72 percent growth. The GroFish™-treated tadpoles had 59 percent growth.

GroFish™ Application With and Without bST on Tadpoles

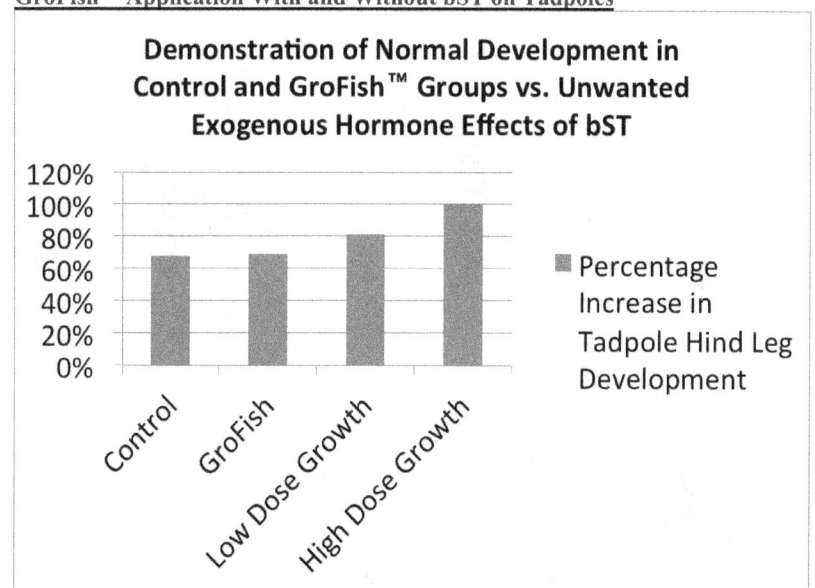

bST had a similar effect as thyroxin on tadpole hind leg development. However, the GroFish™-treated group exhibited similar growth to the bST-treated tadpoles, but with normal hind leg development.

GROFISH TREATMENTS

The GroFish™ Process: Effects on an Animal Cell

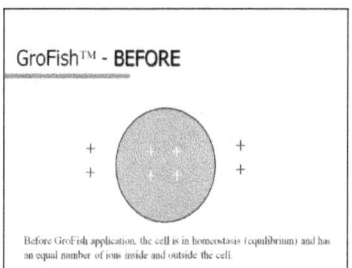

GroFish™ - **BEFORE**

Before GroFish application, the cell is in homeostasis (equilibrium) and has an equal number of ions inside and outside the cell.

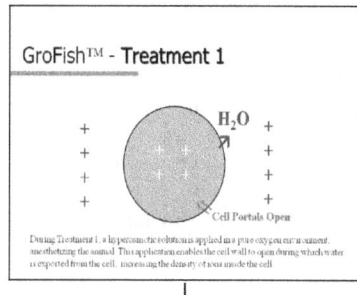

GroFish™ - **Treatment 1**

During Treatment 1, a hyperosmotic solution is applied in a pure oxygen environment, anesthetizing the animal. This application enables the cell wall to open during which water is exported from the cell, increasing the density of ions inside the cell.

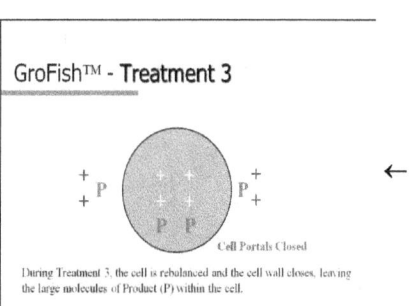

GroFish™ - **Treatment 3**

During Treatment 3, the cell is rebalanced and the cell wall closes, leaving the large molecules of Product (P) within the cell.

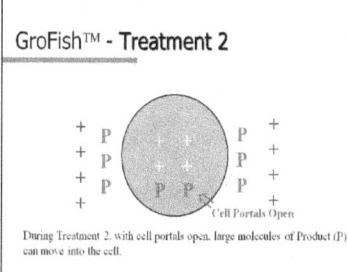

GroFish™ - **Treatment 2**

During Treatment 2, with cell portals open, large molecules of Product (P) can move into the cell.

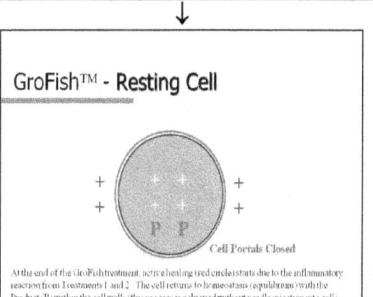

GroFish™ - **Resting Cell**

At the end of the GroFish treatment, active healing (red circle) starts due to the inflammatory reaction from Treatments 1 and 2. The cell returns to homeostasis (equilibrium) with the Product (P) within the cell walls (this process is achieved without needle injection into cell).

Chapter 17. Aquacultural Feed Applications

Proteins are a significant part of aquacultural feed. However, a majority of these proteins end up as pollutants to downstream ecosystems. Utilizing more-efficient delivery systems and molecularly modified feeds can improve metabolism and absorption for the farmed species while also reducing the downstream effects of the unused/effluent product.

Aquaculture Effluent Effects

Aquaculture—also known as fish or shellfish or seafood farming—refers to the breeding, rearing, and harvesting of plants and animals in all types of water environments including ponds, rivers, lakes, and the ocean. Aquaculture produces food fish, sport fish, bait fish, ornamental fish, crustaceans, mollusks, algae, sea vegetables, and fish eggs, which are grown to market size in ponds, tanks, cages, or raceways (NOAA, 2013).

Aquaculture is intertwined with the natural production system through nutrients, pollutants, pathogens, release levels affecting wild stocks, economic research, and public awareness.

Marine aquaculture can take place in the open ocean or inland systems such as ponds or tanks; freshwater aquaculture takes place primarily in ponds and in land-based recirculating aquaculture systems (NOAA, 2013).

According to the United Nations Food and Agriculture Organization (FAO), most of the stocks of the top ten species, which account in total for about 30 percent of world marine capture fisheries production, are fully exploited and, therefore, have no potential for increases in production, while some stocks are overexploited and increases in their production may be possible if effective rebuilding plans are put in place. The declining global marine catch over the last few years together with the increased percentage of overexploited fish stocks and the decreased proportion of non-fully exploited species around the world convey the strong message that the state of world marine fisheries is worsening and has had a negative impact on fishery production. Overexploitation not only causes negative ecological consequences, but it also reduces fish production, which further leads to negative social and economic consequences. To increase the contribution of marine fisheries to the food security, economies, and well-being of the coastal communities, effective management plans must be put in place to rebuild overexploited stocks. The situation seems more critical for some highly migratory, straddling, and other fishery resources that are exploited solely or partially in the high seas (FAO, 2012).

In 2011, global fish consumption hit a record high of 37 pounds per person per year, even though global fish stocks have continued to decline. On average, people eat four times as much fish now than they did in 1950. Around 85 percent of global fish stocks are overexploited, depleted, fully exploited, or in recovery from exploitation (Vince, 2012). Demand for seafood continues to rise as the world's population and human lifespan increases. Benefits of aquaculture include (FAO, 2013):

- Aquaculture can directly contribute to hunger alleviation and urban food security.
- Aquaculture also contributes to urban food security by providing employment and, therefore, income with which food can be purchased.
- Aquaculture contributes to national fiscal balance, including paying taxes, thereby contributing to government revenues.
- Aquaculture can also be a source of hard currency in the form of export dollars.
- When located in isolated rural areas, aquaculture can bring about improved infrastructure, promote the development of small communities, and discourage youth from migrating to cities.

Disadvantages of aquaculture include (FAO, 2013):

- Aquaculture can lead to environmental damage, which can be a major cost to society.
- Commercial and rural aquaculture systems might become competitive rather than complementary.

Aquaculture is a most problematic type of farming in that is has spread nonnative or specially bred species from escapes from ponds or cages, that it provides a great degree of nutrient pollution from excessive feeding and waste products, it enables the clearing of environmentally sensitive land to create ponds for aquaculture and that it is exploitative of many small ocean fish species that may not be sustainable for creation of fish meal and fish oils that are necessary for aquaculture feed production.

When practiced sustainably, aquaculture can benefit the environment by reducing pressure from commercial fishing and has been used to rebuild wild populations. Aquaculture often in developing countries is practiced by many small-scale producers, enhancing local employment and quality of life. Aquaculture also contributes to local food security and generates income.

A growing aquaculture sector has the potential to decrease the pressure on wild fish stocks, provided that market demand for farmed fish is as great as the demand for wild fish (Duke University, 2013).

For an aquaculture site to be permitted, the operation must show that it will maintain a healthy environment for wild animals in the environment, the animals on the farm, and the surrounding habitat. Many environmental factors are evaluated before a farm is permitted and continue to be monitored while the farm is in operation. Such factors include nutrient discharge, protection against escapes of farmed animals, protocols for maintaining fish health, potential impacts to the benthic environment, and many others (NOAA, 2013).

Aquaculture effluents are liquid wastes that are discharged into a body of water. The wastes contain not only solid wastes from the fish, but also nitrogen, phosphorus, and even antibiotics, depending upon the feed used. Aquaculture requires clean water in order to keep fish alive, which means that water changes must be done frequently. The water released can have detrimental effects upon the surrounding environment if not properly handled. Sustainable aquaculture methods, which reduce effluents, are critical to nullifying these effects (Summerfelt and Clayton, 2003).

Reducing Effluents

Aquaculture effluents contain dissolved and suspended solids that have biochemical oxygen demands. Nutrients including phosphorus and nitrogen that are derived from fish excretion, feces, and uneaten feed are the cause of eutrophication. The amount of pollutive effluents results in differences between culture systems, production rates and timing, quantity and quality of source and recipient waters hydraulic retention time, fish species and age, feed types and feeding rates, and management procedures such as cleaning and effluent treatment (Summerfelt and Clayton, 2003).

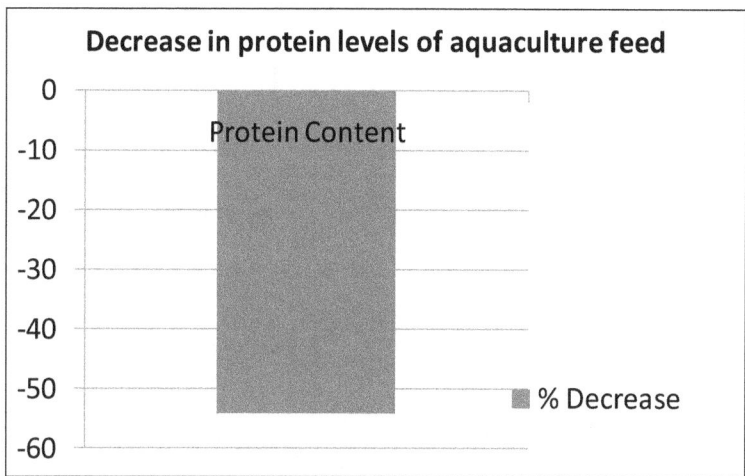

In aquaculture, many species of fish depend on a diet of artificial feed in pellet form. This feed is cast onto the surface of the water and is consumed by the fish as it settles through the water column. Because not all the feed is eaten, a great deal of feed can reach the bottom, where it is eaten by the benthos or decomposed by microorganisms. This alteration of the natural food web structure can significantly impact the local environment (Emerson, 2013).

The impact of aquaculture pond effluents on the environment can be reduced by using relatively simple management practices (Southern Regional Aquaculture Center, 1998):

- Use high-quality feeds and efficient feeding practices.
- Provide adequate aeration and circulation of pond water.
- Minimize water exchange.
- Operate ponds for several years without draining.
- Capture rainfall to reduce pond overflow.
- Allow solids to settle before discharging water.
- Reuse water that is drained from ponds.
- Optimize watershed areas.
- Treat effluents by using constructed wetlands.
- Use effluents to irrigate terrestrial crops.

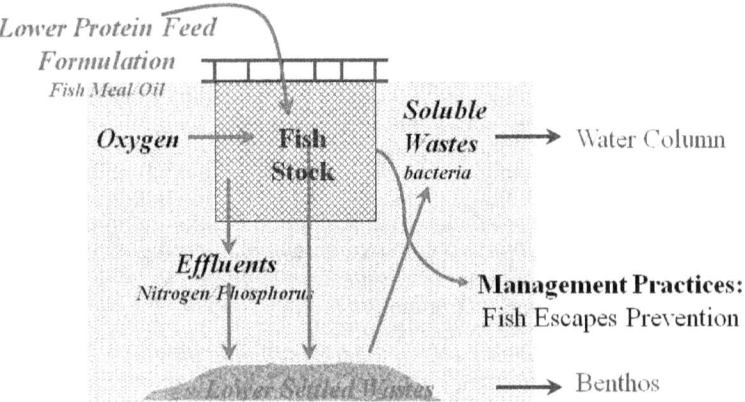

Chapter 18. Conclusion and What You Can Do

In this book, we have laid out a detailed analysis of how the cell works and presented a new theory that the cell is not controlled by the nucleus, but rather by the cell membrane. We have shown the logic of this mechanism for modulation of immunity, nutritional status, transmission from extracellular status to intercellular delivery, and the data supporting this new theory. When using this mechanistic understanding of this new metabolic pathway for plants and animals, it necessitates a change in most formulations for improved active-ingredient action of the products we use for nutrition, cosmetics, animal and plant culture, and health. To improve cellular action, the ionic consistency of the active ingredient(s) needs to balance with the intracellular status. Furthermore, if the desired active ingredient for intracellular transmission is larger than the normal-size pore of the cell being targeted, then a transitory delivery mechanism needs to be employed. BOOSTER™ is such a mechanism. Results from independent laboratory trials show that BOOSTER™'s delivery methodology can yield ten times the absorption of large-molecule products into the cell for metabolic transmission. Additional studies for the past twenty years have shown that GroFish™'s ionic assaults to the cell wall can stimulate improved cell states such as immunity, growth, hormonal, and energy status. This translates to improved methods of agriculture and aquaculture. Indeed, this methodology can deliver healthier animals and more nutritious food products and also be beneficial to the environment. We, as consumers, can participate in this health and sustainability revolution by demanding that the products we eat and use for wellness and cosmetics include BOOSTER™ and GroFish™ technology.

About the Author

Leonard Sonnenschein has over forty-eight years' experience in keeping fish, thirty-seven years' experience in scientific research, twenty-five years' experience in science education innovation, and over one hundred publications and extensive performance in conservation collaboration, climate change issues, and public awareness.

During the first part of Leonard's career, he managed a medical research laboratory during which time he delved further into the bio-physiology of cells, looking at the effect of various solutions on electrical potentials of stomach cells. The research animals used were larval salamanders. These animals would often get diseases, which were also effectively treated after many trials with salt, and the health of the animals' cells when they were treated was improved by the presence of salt in special proportion.

From 1992 to the present, Leonard has been the CEO of the World Aquarium in St. Louis, Missouri USA. Research on over thirty species of aquatic creatures has shown that exposing aquatic species to salt solutions improves their health, growth, and immunosurveillance, and that delivery of large molecules into the cell without injection can be enhanced (Sonnenschein, Leonard, Method of stimulating growth in aquatic animals, US Patent 6,238,706, issued May 29, 2001). Due to the results in fish, Leonard considered mammalian applications as a next step. In 2011, he began looking into the human applications of this technology, and an independent study proved an improvement of 9.6 times in absorption of vitamin D_3 using this technique (Sonnenschein, Leonard, Methods and compositions for enhancing the uptake of an active ingredient, US Provisional Application #61/716331, filed October 17, 2012). It was found to be effective for improved absorption of vitamins, in cosmetic uses, and in radioactive metal removal.

Leonard Sonnenschein is the coauthor and advisor for "New Mechanisms to Understanding the Cell Membrane's Role in Modulating Intercellular Metabolism for Nutritional Delivery," which is a joint program with the Swedish University of Agricultural Sciences, Department of Animal Nutrition and Management, Uppsala, Sweden.

With the results in for many different types of applications of the BOOSTER™ and GroFish™ patented processes, it is clear that Leonard has found a new mechanistic understanding of the cell wall that can be beneficial to consumers from the nutritional, medicinal, and beauty aspects.

Bibliography by Chapter

Preface

1. Guallar, Eliseo, Saverio Stranges, Cynthia Mulrow, Lawrence J. Appel, Edgar R. Miller, III; "Enough Is Enough: Stop Wasting Money on Vitamin and Mineral Supplements." *Annals of Internal Medicine.* 2013 Dec;159(12):850-851.

2. Kamangar, Farin, and Ashkan Emadi. "Vitamin and Mineral Supplements: Do We Really Need Them?." National Center for Biotechnology Information. http://www.ncbi.nlm.nih.gov/pmc/articles/PMC3309636/ (accessed December 19, 2013).

3. Offit, Paul. "The Atlantic." The Atlantic. http://www.theatlantic.com/health/archive/2013/07/the-vitamin-myth-why-we-think-we-need-supplements/277947/ (accessed December 18, 2013).

Chapter 1

4. "Pharmaceutical Industry." *World Health Organization.* Web. 24 Nov. 2013. <http://www.who.int/trade/glossary/story073/en/>.

5. "Transparency Market Research Blog." *Nutraceuticals Product Market Is Expected to Reach USD 204.8 Billion Globally in 2017.* Web. 26 Nov. 2013. <http://www.tmrblog.com/2012/03/nutraceuticals-product-marketglobal.html#sthash.fRoyCKXI.dpuf>.

6. "Global Nutrition Market, Obesity and World Health." *Global Sherpa.* Web. 26 Nov. 2013. <http://www.globalsherpa.org/nutrition-market-obesity-malnutrition>.

7. "Transparency Market Research Blog." *Nutraceuticals Product Market Is Expected to Reach USD 204.8 Billion Globally in 2017.* Web. 26 Nov. 2013. <http://www.tmrblog.com/2012/03/nutraceuticals-product-marketglobal.html#sthash.fRoyCKXI.dpuf>.

8. Animal Facility and Bioanalytical and Pharmacokinetic Analysis Facility, GVK Biosciences Pvt. Ltd. Biology Division, 28 A, IDA, Nacharam, Hyderabad 500 079 India.

9. Miko, Ilona. "Cell Biology." *Nature.com*. Nature Publishing Group. Web. 22 Oct. 2013. <http://www.nature.com/scitable/topic/cell-biology-13906536>.

10. *Vitamin and mineral requirements in human nutrition*. 2nd ed. Geneva: World Health Organization; Food and Agricultural Organization of the United Nations, 2004. Print. http://whqlibdoc.who.int/publications/2004/9241546123.pdf

11. Aubrey, Allison. "For Mind and Body: Study Finds Mediterranean Diet Boosts Both." *NPR*. NPR. Web. 8 Nov. 2013. <http://www.npr.org/blogs/thesalt/2013/11/05/242994376/for-mind-body-study-finds-mediterranean-diet-boosts-both?sc=17&f=1001>.

Chapter 2

12. Bennett, Albert. "Structural and Functional Determinates of Metabolic Rate." Web. 8 Nov. 2013. <https://eee.uci.edu/courses/bio112/bennett.htm>.

13. Cote, Gary, and Mario De Tullio. "Cell Origins and Metabolism." *Nature.com*. Nature Publishing Group. Web. 8 Nov. 2013. <http://www.nature.com/scitable/topic/cell-origins-and-metabolism-14122694>.

14. Martin, L. B., E. Andreassi, W. Watson, and C. Coon. Stress and Animal Health: Physiological Mechanisms and Ecological Consequences. Nature Education Knowledge 3(2011):11. Accessed at http://www.nature.com/scitable/knowledge/library/stress-and-animal-health-physiological-mechanisms-and-23672697.

15. Purdue University. "Researcher lights the way to better drug delivery." Phys.org. 8 Sep 2006. http://phys.org/news76947431.html.

16. "An Introduction to Energy, Enzymes and Metabolism." *McGraw-Hill*. Web. 8 Nov. 2013. <http://highered.mcgraw-hill.com/sites/dl/free/0077290801/787994/sample_chapter06.pdf>.

17. "Chapter 1: Cell Injury, Cell Death & Adaptations." *Elsevier Health*. Elsevier Health. Web. 8 Nov. 2013. <http://www.eu.elsevierhealth.com/media/us/samplechapters/978141602 9731/Chapter%2001.pdf>.

18. Rajendran, Lawrence, Hans-Joachim Knolker, and Kai Simons. "Subcellular targeting strategies for drug design and delivery," Nature Reviews Drug Discovery, Nature Publishing Group. 29-42 (January 2010). doi:10.1038/nrd2897. Accessed at http://java-srv1.mpi-cbg.de/publications/getDocument.html?id=8a8182da2688f245012693a2d 75b0018.

19. "Innate immune system." *Wikipedia*. Wikimedia Foundation, 30 Oct. 2013. Web. 8 Nov. 2013. <http://en.wikipedia.org/wiki/Innate_immune_system>.

20. Sonnenschein, L.A.: "The effects of various physiologic stresses on C3H mice with the Bittner oncologic virus tumor." Transactions of the Missouri Academy of Science 13:209, 1979.

Chapter 3

21. "Nutrient Digestion and Absorption." *Purdue University*. Web. 8 Nov. 2013. <http://web.ics.purdue.edu/~smills/ANSC230/Digestive%20Physiology/ Absorption.html>.

22. Rajendran, Lawrence, Hans-Joachim Knolker, and Kai Simons. "Subcellular targeting strategies for drug design and delivery," Nature Reviews Drug Discovery, Nature Publishing Group. 29-42 (January 2010), doi:10.1038/nrd2897. Accessed at http://java-srv1.mpi-cbg.de/publications/getDocument.html?id=8a8182da2688f245012693a2d 75b0018.

23. McDaniel, Byrd. "Ways Nutrients Are Absorbed in Plants & Animals." *eHow*. Demand Media, 21 Apr. 2011. Web. 8 Nov. 2013.

<http://www.ehow.com/info_8270095_ways-nutrients-absorbed-plants-animals.html#ixzz2jJzIc2sq>.

24. "A-level Biology/Biology Foundation/cell membranes and transport." *Wikibooks, open books for an open world.* Web. 8 Nov. 2013. <http://en.wikibooks.org/wiki/A-level_Biology/Biology_Foundation/cell_membranes_and_transport>.

25. Drake, Victoria. "Linus Pauling Institute Micronutrient Research for Optimum Health." *Linus Pauling Institute at Oregon State University.* Web. 11 Nov. 2013. <http://lpi.oregonstate.edu/ss07/inflammation.html>.

Chapter 4

26. "How Does the Body Absorb Carbohydrates, Fats and Proteins?" *LIVESTRONG.COM.* Web. 8 Nov. 2013. <http://www.livestrong.com/article/489260-how-does-body-absorb-carbohydrates-fats-and-proteins/#ixzz2iUBijHgk>.

Chapter 5

27. Mangete, E.D.O., David West, and C.D. Blankson. "Hypertonic saline solution for wound dressing," *The Lancet,* 28 November 1992 (340, 8831: 1351). doi: 10.1016/0140-6736(92)92533-L.

Chapter 6

28. Animal Facility and Bioanalytical and Pharmacokinetic Analysis Facility, GVK Biosciences Pvt. Ltd. Biology Division, 28 A, IDA, Nacharam, Hyderabad 500 079 India.

29. Rajendran, Lawrence, Hans-Joachim Knolker, and Kai Simons. "Subcellular targeting strategies for drug design and delivery," Nature Reviews Drug Discovery, Nature Publishing Group. 29-42 (January 2010). doi:10.1038/nrd2897. Accessed at http://java-srv1.mpi-cbg.de/publications/getDocument.html?id=8a8182da2688f245012693a2d75b0018.

Chapter 7

30. "The Digestive System and How It Works." *National Institute of Diabetes and Digestive and Kidney Diseases*. Web. 11 Nov. 2013. <http://digestive.niddk.nih.gov/ddiseases/pubs/yrdd/Digestive_System_508.pdf>.

31. "Diffusion, Osmosis, and Movement across a Membrane." *Diffusion*. University of Illinois at Chicago. Web. 11 Nov. 2013. <http://www.uic.edu/classes/bios/bios100/lectures/diffusion.htm>.

32. Lodish ,H., A. Berk, S.L. Zipursky, et al. *Molecular Cell Biology*. 4th edition. New York: W. H. Freeman, 2000. Section 15.8, "Osmosis, Water Channels, and the Regulation of Cell Volume." Available from: http://www.ncbi.nlm.nih.gov/books/NBK21739/.

33. "How Healthy Nutrition Builds Health, Starting With the Cells." *George Mateljan Foundation*. Web. 12 Nov. 2013. <http://www.whfoods.com/genpage.php?dbid=19&tname=faq>.

34. Kaczkowski, Crystal Heather. "Acid-Base Balance Health Article." *Acid Base Equilibrium*. The Gale Group Inc. Web. 25 Nov. 2013. <http://health.yahoo.net/galecontent/acid-base-balance>.

35. "Fluid, Electrolyte, and Acid-Base Balance." Georgia Highlands College. Web. 25 Nov. 2013. <http://www.highlands.edu/academics/divisions/scipe/biology/faculty/harnden/2122/notes/fluelect.htm>.

Chapter 8

36. Hanekamp and Bast. "New recommended daily allowances: benchmarking healthy European micronutrient regulation." *Env. Liability* 4 (2007). http://www4.dr-rath-foundation.org/NHC/studien_pdf/new/New_RDAs_-_Benchmarking_EU_Regulation_-_Bast-Hanekamp_EL_07_4.pdf.

37. "Vitamins and Minerals: How Much Do You Need?" *WebMD*. WebMD. Web. 12 Nov. 2013. <http://www.webmd.com/vitamins-and-supplements/lifestyle-guide-11/vitamins-minerals-how-much-should-you-take>.

38. "How to maximise absorption." *Nutrition Courses, Nutritional Therapy*. Web. 12 Nov. 2013. <http://www.ion.ac.uk/information/onarchives/maximiseabsorption>.

39. Rajendran, Lawrence, Hans-Joachim Knolker, and Kai Simons. "Subcellular targeting strategies for drug design and delivery," Nature Reviews Drug Discovery, Nature Publishing Group. 29-42 (January 2010). doi:10.1038/nrd2897. Accessed at http://java-srv1.mpi-cbg.de/publications/getDocument.html?id=8a8182da2688f245012693a2d75b0018.

40. Casiday, Rachel, and Regina Frey. "Nutrients and Solubility." *Nutrient Solubility*. Web. 12 Nov. 2013. <http://www.chemistry.wustl.edu/~edudev/LabTutorials/Vitamins/vitamins.html>.

41. Harvard Health Publications. *Listing of vitamins*. Harvard Medical School. Web. 25 Nov. 2013. <http://www.health.harvard.edu/newsweek/Listing_of_vitamins.htm>.

42. Broder, Joanna. "Magnesium May Improve Memory." *WebMD*. WebMD. Web. 12 Nov. 2013. <http://www.webmd.com/brain/news/20100127/magnesium-may-improve-memory>.

43. Walton, Bart. "Calcium vs. magnesium: The key is balance." *PCC Natural Markets*. Web. 12 Nov. 2013. <http://www.pccnaturalmarkets.com/sc/0403/sc0403-expertadv.html>.

44. Institute of Medicine (US) Food and Nutrition Board. Dietary Reference Intakes: A Risk Assessment Model for Establishing Upper Intake Levels for Nutrients. Washington, DC: National Academies Press, 1998. "What are Dietary Reference Intakes?" available from: http://www.ncbi.nlm.nih.gov/books/NBK45182/.

45. Council, Subcommittee on Metabolism Staff. *Recommended Dietary Allowances*. 10th ed. Washington: National Academies Press, 1989. Print.

46. Campbell, J. A., and A. B. Morrison. "Some Factors Affecting the Absorption of Vitamins." *Am J Clin Nutr* 12(1963):162-169.

47. Layton, Julia. "Discovery Health." *Discovery Fit and Health*. Web. 25 Nov. 2013. <http://health.howstuffworks.com/wellness/food-nutrition/vitamin-supplements/body-absorb-vitamins.htm>

48. Grady, T.P., Sonnenschein, L.A. and Cheung, L.Y.: Intracellular microelectrode studies of Necturus antral gastric mucosa: electrical potentials and resistances. *Surgical Forum* 33:153, 1982.

49. Cheung, L.Y. and Sonnenschein, L.A.: Intracellular microelectrode studies of Necturus antral mucosa: site of sodium absorption. *Surgical Forum* 34: 158-159, 1983.

50. "Health A-Z." *Daily Omega-3s Recommended for Heart.* N.p., n.d. Web. 13 Jan. 2014. <http://www.m.webmd.com/a-to-z-guides/news/20090803/daily-omega-3s-recommended-heart>.

51. "Mediterranean diet: A heart-healthy eating plan." *Mediterranean diet for heart health.* N.p., n.d. Web. 6 Jan. 2014. <http://www.mayoclinic.org/mediterranean-diet/art-20047801>.

52. "Omega-3 fatty acids." *University of Maryland Medical Center.* N.p., n.d. Web. 13 Jan. 2014. <http://umm.edu/health/medical/altmed/supplement/omega3-fatty-acids>.

53. "Omega-3 Fatty Acids." *Whole Foods.* N.p., n.d. Web. 6 Jan. 2014. <http://www.whfoods.com/genpage.php?tname=nutrient&dbid=84>.

54. Simopoulos AP. "The importance of the ratio of omega-6/omega-3 essential fatty acids." Biomed Pharmacother. 2002 Oct;56(8):365-79.

Chapter 9

55. Russell, Richard. "Why cosmetics are used the way they are." *Why Cosmetics Work.* Web. 12 Nov. 2013. <http://public.gettysburg.edu/~rrussell/Russell_SocialVision_cosmetics_chapter.pdf>

56. "Market Research Reports." *Global Beauty Care Products Industry 2012-2017.* Web. 12 Nov. 2013. <http://www.lucintel.com/reports/consumer_goods/global_beauty_care_p roducts_industry_2012-2017_trend_profit_and_forecast_analysis_september_2012_.aspx>.

57. Schulz, Cory. "Cosmetics Industry—Statistics & Facts | Statista." *Statista RSS.* Web. 12 Nov. 2013. <http://www.statista.com/topics/1008/cosmetics-industry/>.

58. Sonnenschein, L.A.: *"Changing the basis of healthcare by improving active ingredient delivery and nutritional supplements through understanding of new cellular mechanisms."* Global Health & Innovation Conference at Yale University, New Haven, Connecticut, USA, April 12-13, 2014.

59. Piccardi, Nathalie, and Patricia Manissier. "Nutrition and nutritional supplementation: Impact on skin health and beauty." National Institutes of Health. http://www.ncbi.nlm.nih.gov/pmc/articles/PMC2836433/ (accessed December 20, 2013).

Chapter 10

60. Purdue University. "Researcher lights the way to better drug delivery." 8 Sept. 2006. Web. 12 Nov. 2013. <http://phys.org/news76947431.html#jCp>.

61. Rajendran, Lawrence, Hans-Joachim Knolker, and Kai Simons. "Subcellular targeting strategies for drug design and delivery," Nature Reviews Drug Discovery, Nature Publishing Group. 29-42 (January 2010). doi:10.1038/nrd2897. Accessed at http://java-srv1.mpi-cbg.de/publications/getDocument.html?id=8a8182da2688f245012693a2d 75b0018.

Chapter 11

62. Chavanpatil, M., Khdair, A., and Panyam, J. "Surfactant-polymer Nanoparticles: A Novel Platform for Sustained and Enhanced Cellular Delivery of Water-soluble Molecules," *Pharmaceutical Research,* 24 4 10.1007/s11095-006-9203-2 http://dx.doi.org/10.1007/s11095-006-9203-2 Kluwer Academic Publishers-Plenum Publishers 2007-04-01.

63. "Traditional Medicine: Definitions." *WHO.* Web. 12 Nov. 2013. <http://www.who.int/medicines/areas/traditional/definitions/en/>.

64. Sonnenschein, L.A. Presented information about Innovative Drug Manufacturing LLC's delivering nutritional value for nutraceuticals at the 4th International Conference on Medicinal Plants and Herbal Products, held at the John Hopkins University Campus, Rockville, Maryland, USA, September 6-8, 2012.

65. Sonnenschein, L.A.: Presentation of "Understanding Cellular Mechanisms" at Santhigiri Ashram, India. October 29, 2013.

Chapter 12

66. Hunt, Patricia. "Toxins All around Us." *Scientific American.* Web. 14 Nov. 2013. <http://www.scientificamerican.com/article.cfm?id=toxins-all-around-us>.

67. Light, John, and Karin Kamp. "What You Need to Know About Fukushima." *BillMoyers.com.* 18 Nov. 2013. Web. 18 Nov. 2013. <http://billmoyers.com/2013/11/15/what-you-need-to-know-about-fukushima/>.

68. Poland, Anastasia. "Fukushima fallout: Should you eat Pacific fish?" MSN News. Web. 18 Nov. 2013. <http://news.msn.com/science-technology/fukushima-fallout-should-you-eat-pacific-fish>.

Chapter 13

69. "What Is Botox" Wikipedia.

Chapter 14

70. Conway, Jill. "College of Medicine—University of Illinois Urbana-Champaign." August, 2000. Web. 14 Nov. 2013. <https://www.med.illinois.edu/m2/pathology/TAReviews/DCL.php>.
71. Koebler, Jason. "Single Gene May Extend Lifespan by 25 Percent." *US News & World Report*, 6 May 2013. Web. 14 Nov. 2013. <http://www.usnews.com/news/articles/2013/05/06/single-gene-may-extend-lifespan-by-25-percent#comments>.
72. Rajendran, Lawrence, Hans-Joachim Knolker, and Kai Simons. "Subcellular targeting strategies for drug design and delivery," Nature Reviews Drug Discovery, Nature Publishing Group. 29-42 (January 2010). doi:10.1038/nrd2897. Accessed at http://java-srv1.mpi-cbg.de/publications/getDocument.html?id=8a8182da2688f245012693a2d75b0018.

Chapter 15

73. Cage, Darnell. "Reduction of Eutrophication and Effluent Pollution through Fertilizer Modification." World Aquarium Internship Program, August 13, 2008.
74. Sykes, Taylor. "Polluting Our One Percent." World Aquarium REAP Program, August 17, 2013.

75. Sonnenschein, L.A.: "Lowering Nitrate Levels in Closed Saltwater Ecosystems," *CORAL Magazine*, Issue 5, 2004.
76. Rule, V.K., Longmore, W. and Sonnenschein, L.A.: The Effects of Sulfur on Nitrate Levels in a Closed Saltwater Ecosystem. 2nd International Conference on Marine Ornamentals, 2001.

77. Sonnenschein. L.A.: "Effective Organic Amelioration of Nitrate and Other Chemicals of the Dead Zone," Mississippi River Basin Nutrients Science Workshop, October 2005.
78. Foster, Taylor. "A Case Study on a Dairy With Herd-wid e Diarrhea and Reduced Milk Production ." California Polytechnic State University. http://digitalcommons.calpoly.edu/cgi/viewcontent.cgi?article=1067&context=dscisp (accessed December 19, 2013).
79. Schroeder, J.W.. "Bovine Mastitis and Milking Management." North Dakota State University. http://www.ag.ndsu.edu/pubs/ansci/dairy/as1129.pdf (accessed December 19, 2013).
80. "From Feed to Milk: Understanding Rumen Function." Dairy Cattle Nutrition (Penn State Extension). http://extension.psu.edu/animals/dairy/health/nutrition/nutrition-and-feeding/rumen-function/from-feed-to-milk-understanding-rumen-function/view (accessed December 19, 2013).
81. "Vitamin and Mineral Nutrition of Grazing Cattle." Oklahoma State University. http://pods.dasnr.okstate.edu/docushare/dsweb/Get/Document-2032/E-861web.pdf (accessed December 19, 2013).
82. Chiba, Lee. "Diet Formulation & Common Feed Ingredients." Animal Nutrition Handbook. http://www.ag.auburn.edu/~chibale/an18dietformingredients.pdf (accessed December 19, 2013).
83. Borah, Sanjib, and Babul Chandra Sarmah. "Micronutrient in Sustainable Animal Production." Engormix.com. http://en.engormix.com/MA-dairy-cattle/nutrition/articles/micronutrient-sustainable-animal-production-t2670/141-p0.htm (accessed December 19, 2013).
84. Weiss, W.P.. "Minerals and Vitamins for Dairy Cows: Magic Bullets or Just Bullets?." Department of Animal Sciences, Ohio Agricultural Research and Development Center. http://www.ansci.cornell.edu/prodairy/HHNC/proceedings/2012/3.Weiss.Manuscript.pdf (accessed December 19, 2013).

Chapter 16

85. Kean, S.: "Innovation at World Aquarium: Scientists Speed Coral Growth," *St. Louis Post-Dispatch*, July 18, 2005.

86. Cressman, K.A., Sonnenschein, L.A. and Longmore, W.J.: "A Study of Coral Nutrition in a Closed Environment." *Aquaculture America 2000 Conference*, 2000.

87. Hodel, E.C., Sonnenschein, L.A. and Longmore, W.J.: "Effects of Organic and Inorganic Levels in Miniature Coral Reef Systems." *Aquaculture America 2000 Conference*, 2000.

88. Sonnenschein, L.A. and Puntenney, P.J.: "Focus on Oceans and Real Change." *Outreach Magazine*. Stakeholder Forum Publication. Published March 23, 2012.

89. Sonnenschein, L.A.: Presentation of "Stock Enhancement for Improved Health and Growth," World Congress on Ocean in Dalian World EXPO Center, China. September 20-23, 2012.

Chapter 17

90. "What Is Aquaculture?" *National Oceanic & Atmospheric Administration*. Web. 14 Nov. 2013.
<http://www.nmfs.noaa.gov/aquaculture/what_is_aquaculture.html>.

91. *The State of World Fisheries and Aquaculture 2012*. Rome: Food and Agriculture Organization of the United Nations, 2012. Print.

92. "Aquaculture Benefits High, if Practiced Sustainably." *VOA*. 2 Nov. 2009. Web. 14 Nov. 2013. <http://www.voanews.com/content/a-13-2009-01-12-voa44-68627202/407507.html>.

93. "Part I. The Context of Commercial Aquaculture." Web. 14 Nov. 2013.
<http://www.fao.org/docrep/005/x9894e/x9894e04.htm>.

94. "Benefits—Aquaculture." Duke University Department of Biology. Web. 14 Nov. 2013.
<http://biology.duke.edu/bio217/2005/ncm3/benefits.htm>.

95. "Aquaculture & the Environment." *National Oceanic & Atmospheric Administration*. Web. 14 Nov. 2013.
<http://www.nmfs.noaa.gov/aquaculture/faqs/faq_aq_environment.html>
.

96. Summerfelt, R.C., and R.D. Clayton, editors. "Aquaculture effluents: overview of EPA guidelines and standards and BMPS for ponds, raceways, and recycle culture systems." Proceedings from the

conference, Ames, Iowa, October 9, 2003. Publication Office, North Central Regional Aquaculture Center, Iowa State University, Ames, Iowa.

97. Emerson, Craig. "Aquaculture Impacts on the Environment." Web. 14 Nov. 2013.
    <http://www.csa.com/discoveryguides/aquacult/overview.php>.

98. "Characterization and Management of Effluents from Aquaculture Ponds in the Southeastern United States." *Southern Regional Aquaculture Center*. July 1998. Web. 14 Nov. 2013.
    <https://srac.tamu.edu/index.cfm/event/getFactSheet/whichfactsheet/138/>.

99. Vince, Gaia. "How the world's oceans could be running out of fish." *BBC Future—Science and Technology*. BBC, 21 Sept. 2012. Web. 15 Nov. 2013. <http://www.bbc.com/future/story/20120920-are-we-running-out-of-fish>.

100. Sonnenschein. L.A.: "Promotion of Organic Methodology and Alternative Low Food Chain Species for Aquaculture Production – Species Selection and Rearing Technologies," World Aquaculture Society Conference, May 2005.

Chapter 18

101. Kuhn, Thomas S. *The Structure of Scientific Revolutions*, 3rd ed. Chicago: The University of Chicago Press, 1996. Print.

102. Sonnenschein, L.A.: Presentation and poster, "Ocean Engineering: Laboratory Research Findings for Enhancing Water Quality, Biodiversity and Species Proliferation for Coastal Waters" at UNEP-GPA's Second Global Conference on Land-Ocean Connections in Montego Bay, Jamaica. October 2-4, 2013.

Index

Acid-base 37, 42

Active ingredient 4, 5, 6, 7, 31, 34, 35, 43, 59, 61, 62, 63, 65, 66, 70, 93, 94

Agriculture(al) 3, 8, 13, 16, 72, 77, 88, 93, 94

Ammonia 72, 73, 74, 80

Aquaculture (al) 3, 78, 79, 80, 81, 88, 89, 90, 91, 93

Bioavailability 39, 43, 50, 51, 63

BOOSTER 5, 7, 8, 28, 29, 31, 33, 34, 35, 36, 59, 60, 61, 62, 64, 65, 66, 69, 70, 71, 72, 77, 78, 93, 94

BOTOX 65, 69

Calcium 9, 38, 42, 47, 51, 52, 53, 54, 55

Cancer 5, 15, 17, 20, 23, 41, 46, 47, 48, 52, 53, 56, 62, 63, 65, 67

Cell injury 17, 18, 19

Cell metabolism 5, 7, 17, 26, 60

Cell membrane 6, 7, 8, 9, 10, 11, 12, 19, 26, 27, 29, 31, 33, 34, 38, 39, 40 ,41, 57, 93, 94

Cell wall 6, 8, 26, 29, 30, 59, 93, 94

Chemotherapy 62, 64, 65

Coral 3, 78, 80, 83

Cosmetics 4, 5, 6, 7, 29, 34, 47, 48, 59, 60, 61, 62, 69, 93, 94

Delivery 4, 5, 7, 8, 12, 16, 19, 34, 35, 38, 40, 44, 47, 48, 52, 57, 59, 63, 65, 66, 69, 71, 88, 93, 94

Disease 5, 13, 14, 15, 17, 18, 19, 20, 23, 37, 38, 41, 43, 46, 47, 48, 49, 50, 51, 54, 57, 67, 71, 72, 74, 78, 79, 80, 94

Endocytosis 19, 20, 39, 40, 71

Energy production 29, 31, 52

Eutrophic 3, 72, 90

Fatty acid 43, 46, 48, 49, 50, 80

Feed(ing) 13, 22, 38, 62, 77, 78, 79, 80, 81, 82, 88, 89, 90, 91

Fertilizer 72, 73, 76, 77

Golgi complex (Golgi apparatus/ Golgi body) 10, 11, 12, 19, 20, 28, 79

GroFish 6, 34, 36, 57, 58, 71, 78, 79, 80, 81, 82, 83, 84, 85, 86, 87, 93, 94

Herbal 65, 66

Immune system 21, 22, 23, 46
Inflammatory response 6, 22, 25, 28
Iron 44, 50, 51, 53, 54, 63, 68, 72, 73, 74, 76

Magnesium 42, 51, 52, 53, 54, 55
Mineral 5, 7, 12, 14, 15, 39, 42, 43, 44, 50, 51, 52, 53, 56, 57
Mitochondria 12, 18, 19, 20, 28 29, 41, 48, 79

Nitrate 72, 73, 74, 75
Nitrite 72, 73, 74, 77
Nucleus 8, 9, 10, 11, 19, 26, 29, 30, 41, 93
Nutrition 5, 7, 8, 13, 14, 15, 16, 29, 43, 57, 65, 94

Oral (by mouth) 8, 35, 44, 56, 65, 66, 67

Pathogen 8, 16, 17, 20, 21, 28, 29, 31, 52, 79, 80, 88
Pollution 72, 76, 78, 79, 81, 89
Production 21, 29, 30, 31, 32, 42, 46, 47, 54, 72, 78, 80, 88, 90
Protein 6, 7, 8, 9, 10, 11, 13, 19, 20, 22, 27, 28, 31, 35, 39, 40, 42, 45, 48, 52, 54, 56, 57, 63, 71, 79, 80, 88

Radioactive 67, 94

Selenium 51, 52, 54, 55, 56
Skin 14, 25, 34, 45, 47, 48, 50, 53, 60, 61, 65, 67, 68, 70
Subcellular delivery 19, 71
Sulfur 56, 72, 73, 74, 75, 76

Topical (transdermal) 61, 62, 65, 66, 69, 70
Toxin 18, 19, 67, 68, 69
Traditional Medicine 65, 66
Transport effect 33

Vitamin 5, 7, 8, 12, 14, 29, 31, 35, 43, 44, 45, 46, 47, 48, 51, 52, 53, 56, 57, 60, 62, 63, 65, 94

Zinc 38, 46, 51, 52, 53, 56

ARTÍCULOS
© Rafael Granizo

ISBN-13: 978-1542868402
ISBN-10: 1542868408

Artículos

Rafael Granizo

He creído conveniente recopilar algunos de mis artículos que definen, además de un ideario socialista, un mundo, hoy ya casi utópico, donde los valores esenciales de dignidad de las personas son vulnerados y despreciados por las enormes fauces de un capitalismo desmedido y al amparo de mediocres personajes protagonistas de la España moderna de principios del siglo XXI. En gran medida, estos artículos, describen el afán infame de personas que, utilizando nobles ideales para beneficio propio, convierten la casa constitucional de todos, en un lodazal.

La cómoda impudicia

Publicado por infoLibre 16/11/2016

Cuántas veces se ha oído decir aquello de que el hombre es una animal de costumbres, ¿verdad? Y cuántas veces nos hemos sentido protagonistas en oráculos terrenales. Somos prototipos vinculantes a una sociedad que nos maneja a capricho porque nosotros mismos la alimentamos con nuestras conductas. Forjamos una sociedad a nuestra imagen y semejanza bien creando rutinas o hábitos y siendo agentes activos de esa construcción, alcanzando así, la condición de ciudadano. Sin embargo, hay dudas en cuanto a esa condición. Ya Aristóteles decía, en el Siglo V a. C. que el ciudadano de una democracia, con frecuencia, no lo sería en una oligarquía y atendiendo a esa reflexión y, observando el hacer político en el Siglo XXI, el uso y caso que nuestros políticos hacen a las demandas de los ciudadanos a través del voto, es evidente que tenemos proporcionalmente de ciudadanos lo que ellos tienen de honrados.

Sin duda somos nosotros quienes les preparamos sus nidos faraónicos con nuestras rutinas y hábitos democráticos. Permitimos con nuestras actuaciones domésticas que gobierne quien más y mejor ha utilizado la desvergüenza y el abuso y contemplamos cómo más que aficionados templarios que dicen llamarse socialistas, modelan a su capricho los votos de sus militantes, arrebatándoles sus banderas de honestidad a cambio de sus miserias para que siga gobernando la concupiscencia y el libertinaje. Por tanto permitimos que se nos siga tratando como meros espectadores en una sala de cine ante una tediosa película de mafiosos; viendo infinitos paseíllos a los juzgados de todo un abanico de de seres indeseables que impunemente, éstos nunca pagarán sus culpas, se siguen paseando libremente como heroicos mecenas de una España humillada, más que por lo que han hecho, por los apoyos ciudadanos que aún tienen. Pero también, y ya ampliando horizontes, ver cómo tras los muros domésticos, identidades democráticas llamadas sociedades avanzadas convierten océanos en cementerios, o permiten ciudades como Alepo o diásporas como las del pueblo Sirio, es desolador. Permítanme solo un recuerdo: Se llamaba Aylán Kurdi y no era un niño, no tuvo tiempo. En cuatro años, sólo vio desesperación y huida, llantos, gritos y lágrimas. No, no le dejaron ser niño, no pudo ser un niño. Se llamaba Aylán Kurdi Y murió ahogado en una playa de Turquía mecido por olas marinas, asfixiado por metralla, por odios y por venganzas... Se llamaba Aylán Kurdi.

Estas sociedades, decía, autistas y mezquinas que para vergüenza, no de todos, sustentan polvorines bélicos amparándose en cómodos privilegios de quienes las gobiernan, son tan miserables que no permiten que se manche su ADN llegando a taponarles la puerta de la dignidad. Esta vergüenza de países a los que estamos unidos no alcanzan, ni mucho menos, el honor de llamarse demócratas por mucho que pronuncien la honrosa palabra, sino que son serviles feudos al servicio de mercados oligárquicos que están por encima de ellas, y donde se prioriza el dinero frente a todo. En su mundo, en nuestro mundo, solo parece existir la impudicia, no importan las enfermedades, desprecian la justicia, odian la educación, se ríen cuando se habla de igualdad, y una retahíla interminable de desprecios a quienes les han convertido en monstruos, en unos perfectos Padrinos de Coppola. Siendo así y volviendo a Aristóteles dudo mucho que podamos llamarnos ciudadanos, tan solo porque muestran, con esa retahíla citada, que les importamos un carajo. No, este traje de ciudadano no me sienta bien, como no me sienta bien, una sociedad que vive en la inopia y en una cómoda impudicia. También, los que nos llamamos ciudadanos somos responsables de ello, nuestros silencios les hace soberbios y alimenta su despotismo. Este traje nos queda demasiado grande a to-dos porque somos ajenos y desmemoriados con aquellos que asentaron bases y valores para una sociedad moderna, amparada en derechos y debe-res que hoy deberíamos defender. Sí, vivimos ins-talados en una cómoda impudicia a la que cada día corremos un tupido velo amparados en hábitos y costumbres banales que van desdibujando el carácter de ciudadano en beneficio de cortesanos con servidumbres indignas.

Palomitas

Publicado por infoLibre 17/10/2016

Era de sentido común, nada extraño y muy necesario. Fue el 15-M el momento en el que una gran mayoría de socialistas, hoy en Podemos, dijo basta ya a un PSOE asentado felizmente a la sombra del Partido Popular y rodeado de mayúsculas prebendas muy alejadas de las miserias y recortes de quienes les votaron.

El maquiavelismo de los barones socialistas, que no son otros que los que alcanzaron la gloria, esto es, los ex ministros, presidentes, diputados... o lo que es lo mismo, esos que llevan viviendo como hedonistas señorías ya mucho tiempo, demostrando con sus actos las virtudes de sus honras, ahogando a muchos ciudadanos para conseguir suculentos bienestares, y tanto es así, que son capaces de utilizar artimañas golpistas para no

13

desprenderse de sus bonanzas, incluyendo como hacen otros, editoriales periodísticas.

Estos seres codiciosos que viven a diario en la abundancia gracias a las miserias que dejan a sus votantes, han llevado al hartazgo de éstos teniendo la desfachatez de buscarse un señuelo para exculparse y culparle, poco menos, que de los males de la humanidad. Achacarle a su víctima el progresivo desastre electoral, es poco menos que reírse de la inteligencia de sus votantes.

No es necesario recordarles que el señor Pedro Sánchez, fue el único secretario general que ha sido elegido por la militancia socialista, eso le debe doler mucho al Ilmo. Sr. D. Felipe, Dios le guarde mucho años. Son Ellos, estos engreídos barones muchos de ellos residuales de otros tiempos, los culpables, con su manifestaciones y hechos, del desánimo de sus votantes. Solo hay que mirar dónde viven ellos y dónde sus bases. Son estas señorías las que utilizando la nobleza del ideario socialista, se han postrado ante el becerro de oro. Sí, era necesario y tenía que pasar, la cohabitación entre nobles parásitos y humildes trabajadores no podía durar más tiempo, además de que era más que previsible, era necesario para la regeneración de un ideal frustrado. Por tanto, bienvenida esta contienda que a buen seguro sólo tendrá un ganador, el socialismo, con independencia de quien salga mejor o peor parado.

Por el momento Pedro Sánchez ya ha caído, pero esto no significa, ni mucho menos, que los golpistas hayan triunfado, solo han mostrado sus virtudes y sus vilezas. Ahora sí, los socialistas, una vez separado el trigo de la cizaña, que decía San Mateo, ejercerán su veredicto. No olvidemos, como he dicho anteriormente, que muchos socialistas están en una casa de acogida expectantes de lo que pase en la 'Casa Madre' y que todos los movimientos de los implicados serán escudriñados al milímetro.

Mensajes o eslóganes del 15-M como *Democracia real ya*, *Lo llaman democracia y no lo es* o lo más denigrante *PSOE y PP la misma mierda es,* no solo fueron los prolegómenos de esta explosión que vivimos hoy, sino que siguen estando vigentes, es el mensaje de un pueblo pidiendo que la cordura vuelva a la política y que se destierre de ella a los indecentes que la utilizan.

Nunca una irresponsabilidad fue tan responsable políticamente hablando, tan elocuente y ejemplarizante, pues a diferencia de otros que en modo alguno penalizan los abusos y la corrupción, los ciudadanos socialistas prefieren, cuando se menosprecian sus ideales, buscar hogares ajenos que agradecen, a veces tanto, que pueden quedarse a vivir toda una vida. Ser socialista es ser paciente e íntegro, tan paciente e íntegro como seguir esperando a que algún día la fraternidad entre las personas deje de ser una quimera. Estemos pues, todos expectantes y rodeémonos de unas palomitas, sí, palomitas como decían los otros, para ver las servidumbres que dejen ver las oquedades de las miserias. Ya vamos teniendo relatos y muestrarios de cómo pueden ser los protocolos del servilismo. Es cuando menos irónico volver a ver versionado por los socialistas el cuento de "El flautista de Hamelín", y ver cómo tras los abducidos animalitos transitan otros seres, éstos críticos, muchos igualmente abducidos por sus editoriales que nos cuentan realidades ya diseñadas.

Es patético observar cómo en nombre de unos ideales tan dignos se quiere aupar al gobierno de un país a un partido que en el mismo momento y hora se le está juzgando por corrupción; una corrupción de la que ya nadie duda. Pero también es cierto que entre tanta mediocridad aparecen figuras que nos muestran aún ascuas de un socialismo vivo y esperanzador, volver a oír voces como las de Pérez Tapias y Borrell es volver a escuchar el crepitar del fuego socialista de otros tiempos. En fin, que sigamos con las palomitas contemplando el desfile actoral que vertebra hoy la casa socialista para decantar el futuro voto. ¡Ah! y no se preocupen por la imagen o las vergüenzas, hay veces que para acabar con los ácaros hay que raparse al cero.

Lo moral, lo inmoral y lo cotidiano

Publicado por infoLibre 01/10/2016

Es en nuestra edad infantil cuando oímos hablar, por primera vez, de las liendres, piojos y garrapatas. Las escuelas infantiles son viveros apropiados para la propagación de estos ácaros. Con ellos llegan los picores, las rascaduras, las espulgaciones, los vinagres y los aceites y mil remedios para acabar con ellos y prevenirnos de sus males. ¡Es la locura en casa! Toda una guerra. Una guerra en torno a unos bichitos que se nutren de nuestro sistema sanguíneo y que nos afecta considerablemente a nuestra cotidianidad, dejándonos en fuera de juego una semana, quizás dos, sin llevar a los niños al colegio, tirando de los abuelos, de los permisos y de quien sea necesario. Hay que aislar al individuo, para aislar al ácaro y poder sanar la enfermedad.

¿Quién no ha tenido, en algún momento, en su familia ácaros? Esta pregunta que si bien parece tener una fácil respuesta, se complica cuando la

19

sometemos al virtuosismo de estos parásitos y de quien los padece en la vida adulta. En esta edad y en este tiempo, ya no hay guerra, ni picores, ni nos rascamos, ni espulgamos, ni usamos aceites, ni siquiera buscamos remedios contra ellos, es más, les ponemos los medios para que sigan chupando de nuestro esfuerzo, de nuestra sangre, conserván-dolos en grandes microclimas para que subsis-tan. La locura pasa a ser cordura, no se pierde tiempo; la ley deja de ser un refugio seguro; ya ni se buscan remedios, ni antídotos, vivimos como simples ciudadanos en otro microclima o burbuja que nos hace ser ajenos a semejantes e incómodos bichitos. Esos microclimas llamados unos, Senado, otros diputaciones y algunos, diócesis... Hay más, pero el artículo no puede ser muy extenso, nos til-da la cara a todos los ciudadanos del color del con-formismo, del aroma de la cobardía, poniéndonos un rictus de felicidad en un océano de vergüenza.

Que no haya antídotos para acabar con garrapatas ancladas en tribunas de oro, que no haya recursos legislativos para espulgar sanguijuelas que llevan cuarenta años chupando, que tengamos un sistema de gobierno amparado en un estado de derecho y que lo permita, es vivir en una burbuja o microclima también enfermo. El virus es ya una pandemia. Todos somos culpables de ello. Yo también.

Habría que nombrar día nacional, aquel 10 de junio de 2003, día del *Tamayazo*, como día de la dependencia. Día en el que el descaro institucional de nuestro estado de derecho abofeteó y convirtió, cual milagro mesiánico, a los crédulos ciudadanos democráticos en incrédulos obreros, hoy casi esclavos, de éstos faraones capaces de fagocitar sus propios piojos por sacar más tajada, y que abundan en nuestra política (véase la escuela valenciana, o madrileña, la andaluza o la catalana). Da ya igual que la escuálida vaca apenas dé leche para tanto ácaro. Sentémonos a esperar la revolución que nos corresponde. Ya la tuvieron los ingleses en 1688, y que, una vez asomados al mundo europeísta han respondido con un brexit; después vinieron los franceses, que andan en las horas más bajas desde la revolución de 1848 coincidiendo, curiosamente, con la unión de estados europeos.

En fin, que estamos cómodamente sentados en el hedor que produce la enfermedad y aunque a veces encontremos, en el fondo de nuestro paladar, algún sabor a almíbar, lo cierto es que, al igual que Sancho Panza, estamos atrapados en la paciencia para con nuestros amos. Sigamos pues remando en dirección a un puerto cada vez más bello por la bruma que lo oculta y dejemos que los brotes verdes, que siempre nos anuncian, sigan brotando en nuestro jardín. Es mi última reflexión y creo entender en ella que lo moral, lo inmoral y lo cotidiano parecen igualarse por el hambre de una sanguijuela.

¡Ah! Se me olvidaba decirles que son las diez y veintitrés minutos y que estoy en el Museo del Prado, observando el cuadro de Goya pintado hacia 1820, *Saturno devorando a un hijo*. Sin duda este Goya fue un adelantado a su tiempo y no precisamente por su pintura. A mi lado, alguien con gafas oscuras, se encorva buscando la firma del autor, dejando ver en el bolsillo trasero del pantalón, una octavilla que dice: Charla-Debate sobre el 15-M por Carl...

Sueños y quimeras del PSOE

Publicado por el Periódico 28/09/2016

Cuanto más hablan, más se desangra la familia socialista. Son obviedades que van dejando un relieve cada día más nítido de quienes utilizan las miserias de unos para satisfacerse. Con tanta elección, el maquiavelismo de los barones socialistas y sus cánticos deshojan, hasta la desnudez, la estructura de un ya falso socialismo muy alejado de su bases ciudadanas.

Estas sirenas Homéricas convertidas en querubines maledicentes que habitan en feudos faraónicos, son seres creados para fagocitar lo poco que va quedando de la rebeldía que pide justicia social. Escuchar sus voces mesiánicas, mientras el Ulises Sánchez y sus hombres, taponando sus oídos y atados al mascarón de proa de una precaria nave socialista intentan eludir los hechizos y las seducciones de los bien llamados barones, es cuanto menos, una escena surrealista que describe la bacanal en la que viven estos nobles que ignoran, no solo a quien eligieron las bases, sino la singularidad del socialismo. Desde mi particular alféizar, contemplar estos cánticos de sirena es poco menos que asistir a un ajuste de cuentas o venganzas donde todos salen convertidos en víctimas.

Más me parece que estas guerrillas obedecen a una estrategia pensada y con propósitos bien definidos que actúan cuando hay elecciones, por ser esa es su cadencia. Es cuando montan sus aquelarres: cantan apenas dos noche, atraen tertulias, amenizan las prensas y desaparecen a sus atalayas a observar cómo sus cánticos homéricos hacen efecto, que no es otro, que contemplar cómo la diáspora de la familia socialista va desangrándose, gota a gota, hacia un fatídico destino. No les hace falta nadie. Siguen siendo poderosos en la sombra. Tan poderosos que prefieren limpiar la casa y quedarse sin servidumbre a pesar de que fueron éstos quienes les auparon.

Falta pues, voces que sean capaces de enfrentarse a ellos y les inviten a tomar la puerta de salida de una casa a la que no hacen honor, que les ponga donde les corresponde, desde luego no al lado del pueblo donde nunca han sabido estar. La orfandad es un mal nunca deseado, pero si es fruto del engaño, bienvenida sea; al menos es lo que dice la sensatez cuando los dirigentes se distancian tanto de las bases que hasta llegan a perder la naturaleza de su ADN.

Falta alguien en el socialismo que acabe con esta diáspora que solo beneficia a los de siempre. Los socialistas siguen estando ahí; son parte esencial en nuestro país, en nuestro mundo. Su pensamiento nos hace iguales a todos en justicia y en libertad, basándose en la fraternidad entre los iguales y los diferentes; es un catálogo, nítido y claro donde todo el mundo civilizado desearía vivir. No, los socialistas no han desaparecido, han emigrado al amparo de otras familias porque quien rige su común casa los ha echado torticeramente con sus políticas arrogantes de desigualdad.

Pero siguen estando, como lo están todos esos exiliados que han tenido que marchar a Europa para poder sobrevivir y labrarse un futuro, pero siempre con la mirada puesta en el posible regreso que les acerque a sus infancias. Es hora de abrir los ojos a bondades que faciliten el retorno al hogar común; es hora de volver a aferrarse a la mano del otro y buscar miradas cómplices para no sentirse solo. La equidad y la justicia social son quimeras que residen en la razón y no en lugares utópicos aunque no lo parezca. Hay sociedades que así lo demuestran. Hay que romper falsos miedos y llamar por su nombre, sea honestidad o traición, las identidades de los hechos. Es hora de sacar de la escena socialista a quienes utilizan máscaras de farsante amparadas en dramaturgias de honestidad ¿Es hora de que el fariseísmo de los mercaderes deje de mancillar el orgullo de los Obreros Españoles.

Es hora de levantarse. Tengo que ir a trabajar. Buenos días.

Hay primaveras que nunca parecen llegar

Publicado por infoLibre 21/09/2016

Cuesta mucho ser paciente con la intolerancia, con la verborrea de algunos comentarios que parecen más producto del adiestramiento cerebral que de reflexiones basadas en el análisis y la experiencia. Escuchar o presenciar aún ofensas e insultos en foros, calles, autobuses y hasta en el mismo parlamento hacia los perdedores de la guerra civil española mina mi carácter. Contemplar como sigue una parte de esta sociedad encerrada en el laurel de la victoria de hace ochenta años, despreciando a las víctimas que quedaron sepultadas o que han crecido con el estigma de la orfandad de sus seres queridos, privados de derechos fundamentales y subyugados a tener que vivir en la esperanza, sigue socavando mi tolerancia. Observar la llegada de nuevas generaciones infectadas con el virus del rencor hacia aquellos que quieren suturar, aunque sea con hilo de rabia, las cicatrices de su memoria me produce cefaleas poco recomendables. Ver cómo las hienas vuelven, una y otra vez, a sacar sus colmillos en torno a la Ley de Memoria Histórica desespera al más paciente y verles aullar en torno a sus presas, con ademanes de crispación, vuelve a helarme la hiel.

Si tras cuarenta años, simples reconocimientos de justicia histórica y social, a quienes vilmente fueron perseguidos, humillados y asesinados, les provoca asombro y estupor es que el franquismo hizo, más que bien, su trabajo de adiestramiento. Hoy viéndoles vestidos de demócratas, de constitucionalistas, escuchando muchos de sus argumentos y observando sus comportamientos siguen provocándome escalofríos. Más me parecen vigías extemporáneos de aquél numeroso puñado de militares que sometieron al pueblo a un genocidio, liberadores de patrias que, aún hoy, siguen ejemplarizando nuestras calles con sus nombres. Ha pasado ya mucho tiempo... Pero en numerosas ocasiones y ante sus argumentos, sigo escuchando el acezar de la sangre de aquellas víctimas ante sus torturadores, la virulencia en sus palabras, el sarcasmo de sus rictus y la felicidad que les provoca su arrogancia. Sí, por momentos estos tiempos me evocan las vilezas de aquellas fieras sobre sus atemorizadas víctimas en oteros de fiesta.

Han pasado cuarenta años tras otros cuarenta años y aquel túnel de temor y miedo parece activo aún. Cuando una sociedad sigue bailando al son de hienas que continúan pateando derechos esenciales en la persona, como es la dignidad, está ante una sociedad enferma en grave estado de ulceración. Expresiones como la de la señora Aguirre: "Es una ley fratricida que el PP debería haber derogado. Una ley absurda" o la del señor Hernando: "Algunos se han acordado de su padre enterrado solo cuando había subvenciones", nos muestra los signos de ulceración a los que he aludido.

Más cae mi desánimo cuando contemplo la inagotable cantera de voceros, tertulianos o periodistas dependientes, que los agasaja diariamente como si se tratara de una guardia falangista. Es mucho tiempo ya el que ha pasado con muy poco bagaje democrático conseguido. Estos vigías extemporáneos de salvadores de patrias pasadas ya llevan mucho tiempo dando coces. La ley de la Memoria Histórica es sólo una de ellas, la propia Constitución Española, en sus 169 artículos ha sido víctima diaria de sus regocijos lúdicos y su despotismo ante la mirada de consternación de aquellos que creyeron salir de aquel viejo túnel de miedo, véase tan solo el otoño judicial que nos espera gracias a ellos; véase sus miedos campando a sus anchas por las mismas aceras que pisamos sus víctimas.

Hay poca esperanza, muy poca y primaveras que nunca parecen llegar... En un país donde los derechos y deberes de los ciudadanos son ninguneados durante tanto tiempo por quienes deben velar por ellos y mantienen esa cuota de votantes fieles a esos desmanes, nunca puede haber orgullo sino resignación. Oírles apelar, diariamente, al patriotismo y al constitucionalismo es, más que una mala broma, el desprecio absoluto a quienes no piensan como ellos.

No, éstos no son políticos, como no lo fueron los otros, son solo becarios de sus mezquindades que ahondan en las entrañas del ciudadano para sacar tajada. No nos engañemos, nuestro sistema político podrá ser llamado democracia pero la etimología de la palabra democracia no se corresponde con la realidad social que vivimos.

Quizá es que uno es excesivamente romántico y crea en quimeras quijotescas o tan solo sean los sueños de un majadero que pretende poner un punto y aparte a un tiempo de paciencia y resignación tan dilatado que nos permita a todo un pueblo caminar en una misma dirección. Permitirme, por último, mostrarles el odio visceral de una mujer que fue perdedora en la guerra civil española en su despedida a un hijo: "*Voy a morir con la cabeza alta... Sólo te pido... que quieras a todos y que no guardes nunca rencor a los que dieron muerte a tus padres, eso nunca. Las personas buenas no guardan rencor... Enrique, que te hagan hacer la comunión, pero bien preparado, tan bien cimentada la religión como me la cimentaron a mí... Hijo, hijo, hasta la eternidad...*". Fueron las últimas palabras escritas de Blanca Brisac, tenía 29 años y fue una de las trece rosas rojas fusilada en

la tapia del Cementerio de la Almudena en la ma-
drugada del cinco de agosto de 1939.

"Si callamos gritarán las piedras"

Publicado por infoLibre 29/08/2016

"Si callamos gritarán la piedras". Esta contundente frase dicha por Jesús, –Lucas 19:40–, en mi humilde opinión sacada de contexto, es la respuesta de reverendísimos obispos ante el sarpullido que les produce la ley pro LGTB, una ley aprobada por el pleno de la Asamblea de Madrid, epicentro de la soberanía popular.

Pues bien, respetando, como no podía ser de otra manera, sus grandilocuentes quejidos y amparado en mi propio sarpullido por la falta de ecuanimidad en casi todo lo que dicen y hacen, haré uso, igualmente, de mi libertad de expresión.

Permítanme, en primer lugar, dudar de mi fariseísmo al dedicarles estas palabras, pues queriendo ser prudente, y teniendo los mismos orígenes – el vientre de una madre– me cuesta, como simple articulista, mirar hacia arriba y escalar sus faraónicas libreas para acceder a verles la cara. Por cierto, henchidas y rosáceas, expresión de buena salud, de lo que sin duda me alegro, pero que curiosamente no siempre coincide con el rostro del pueblo al que ustedes destinan sus epístolas.

Asimismo, quiero pedirles de antemano su indulgencia a mi osadía, pues me cuesta dirigirme a ustedes. Créanme, uno sabe poco de ilustres ciudadanos que proclaman la palabra de dios metidos en la sencillez de unos protocolos tan ajenos al raciocinio y tan grandilocuentes. Reverendísimos, Muy ilustres, Ilustrísimos, Eminentísimos... No parece que habiten ustedes en la humildad y en la sencillez. Más diría yo, parece que ustedes, con sus reprimendas, residen en el reino de la soberbia. Eso de añadir los "ísimos" me produce estornudos, permítanme la arrogancia y perdónenme si me equivoco, pero parece más propio de militares a los que se les quedaba pequeña la graduación de general, hoy residentes en mausoleos con bóvedas quijotescas que parecen querer representar, más que la subida al reino de los cielos, el asalto a éste, con ascensión de todo tipo de material bélico, incluido tanques.

En fin, que no quiero desconfiar de sus buenas intenciones, pero permítanme una vez más que tras escuchar su arenga, discrepe en su hacer y proceder, pues la piedra lanzada al aire, muchas veces, le cae a uno encima, y si no, vean lo que les dice el sumo sacerdote de la iglesia: " ...Les ruego no caigan en la paralización de dar viejas respuestas a nuevas demandas. ¡Ay de ustedes si se duermen en los laureles!". Y ni que decir tiene si leemos a Mateo –21:12-13– respecto de las palabras de Jesús en el templo de Jerusalén.

Les ruego pónganse un ratito frente a un espejo con todos sus abalorios eclesiásticos –la mitra, el palio, el anillo, el báculo, la gran cruz en el pecho– y observen un minuto la humildad de sus bordados. Luego busquen al nazareno, con minúsculas, sencillo con una simple túnica, sin don que abrigue su nombre, sin homilías que anuncien siniestras plagas, sin belenes de más de un millón de euros, sin falsas dádivas que sufraguen el uso de su palabra, sin codicias patrimoniales... Creo, eminencias, que ustedes han equivocado una vez más el sermón, tachando con maledicencia una ley aprobada por los representantes de la soberanía popular que está basada en el respeto. Más vale que pongan sus alaridos en sus propios quehaceres, pues las bondades que muestran son ajenas a una ciudadanía cada día más alejada de su arrogancia. La evolución de los pueblos provienen de sus propias necesidades, de sus propias exigencias pero, sobre todo, de lo que esté dispuesto a exigirse, y no así de custodias de conciencias que no evolucionan, que solo son dunas de arena que dificultan el caminar de las sociedades.

Este tipo de comportamientos medievales que tienen como objetivo culturizar a un pueblo no deja de ser un insulto a la inteligencia, pues una cultura que oprime nunca puede ser llamada cultura, por muchos sermones que ofrezcan o por cientos de emisoras que las prediquen. Vaya pues mi profana reprimenda a quienes se esconden en oteros demasiado elevados para menospreciar nuevas libertades y callar continuamente los abusos y desprecios de los poderes que les apadrinan.

Crispín en busca de una nueva viñeta

Publicado por infoLibre 20/08/2016

En primer lugar, permítanme hacer un breve homenaje póstumo a quien tantos momentos de bienestar y ocio me ha dado en la infancia, el escritor Víctor Mora, creador, entre otros personajes, de *El Jabato* y el *Capitán Trueno* y, por ende, padre de mi tertuliano Crispín. Vaya por él mi absoluto respeto y admiración, y también este artículo, que tiene mucho que ver con personajes, aventuras y política.

Crispín vuelve a la carga. Amparado en la majadería de un pacto entre los constitucionalistas, me sorprende que este hombre haya estudiado Derecho, pues más parece que estudió torcido, porque llamar constitucionalista al actual partido en el Gobierno, sabedores ya de sus incontables abusos y desmanes, es la mayor tropelía que he oído a un político, y eso que su Capitán Trueno, cada vez que abre la boca, además de ponernos los ojos como mayúsculas conteniendo en su centro, también, grandes símbolos de admiración e interrogación unidos, nos deja un buen puñado de frases para el registro en un archivo de humor.

Perdonen, vuelvo a hilar, como decía mi hijo: "Padre, vuelve al hilo que te pierdes". Como decía, amparado en ese mal llamado constitucionalismo, vuelve a ser el protagonista central de la escena política española, para repartir vituperios a diestro y siniestra y otorgarse elogios y bondades a sí mismo, en forma de oro olímpico, subiéndose, apoyado en sí mismo, a lo más alto del podio, enarbolando la bandera rojigualda de España y mostrándonos a todos los españoles la magnanimidad de su obra, el único camino posible para poder salir de la crisis que ellos, sus contertulios sociales y políticos, crearon para arrebatar cuales corsarios las prebendas a sus cortesanos. Prebendas, bien sea dicho, que fueron dadas por ellos, que no, innatas.

Vuelve Crispín a las andadas. Primero el pacto con los señores que abrazaron la curia de la justica social ¡por España y para España!; después vino Venezuela, no sé si quiso emular a Colón en su tercer viaje y redescubrirla teniendo sus minutos de gloria, que sin duda les supieron a poco porque, más tarde, ya habiendo emulado mil veces a Simón Pedro en el evangelio, negando ante toda su España su afinidad con el Capitán Trueno, quiso que éste se sometiera a unas directrices que para cualquier ciudadano son obvias; y ahora nos muestra, bajo sus pies, la reconversión humillante de su Capitán. ¿Se restablecerá el Capitán Trueno, o será decapitado por su amigo Crispín? ¿Qué nos esperará en el siguiente episodio?

Ayer leía a Pablo Simón decir que un estudio científico concluye que ser mejor que los demás mejora la autoestima. Bien, este Crispín, sin duda, tiene la autoestima muy, pero que muy alta, tanto, que nuestro particular salvador de patrias, cree ya ir en un anda.

– ¡Padre, te has vuelto a ir!

– Pues sí, hijo. Los vericuetos del raciocinio a veces me juegan malas pasadas, hacen del hombre justo un juicio injusto y este Crispín, cada vez que sale a la palestra, convierte mis cavilaciones en majaderías, ¿o no? En fin hijo, el estío es una muy buena temporada para oír el chirriar de las cigarras...

– Definitivamente te has ido, padre... Y hazme el favor, no me mezcles en tus delirios.

El político cuántico

Publicado por infoLibre 14/08/2016

Casi cuarenta años llevamos oyendo hablar de las bondades y las veleidades de nuestro sistema político constitucional, y son muchos los adjetivos utilizados para definir los claroscuros de su trayectoria. Un análisis moderado de esta cuestión nos apunta una complicada cohabitación de conciencias y sus respectivas metamorfosis una vez alcanzan el poder. Es aquí donde la expresión latina *rara avis* nos muestra la sorprendente figura del político cuántico y sus mutaciones.

El caso más común anida en la tan denostada doctrina socialista. Sería interminable la lista de políticos en nuestra trayectoria democrática que, utilizando como fuente de energía las ideas socialistas, acaban abrazando el destellante mundo del poder y del dinero, convirtiéndose en perfectos conservadores de su botín. Hay ejemplos tan obvios que los voy a omitir. Pero si bien no son comparables, al menos en cantidad, también hay fenómenos que transitan en sentido contrario, esto es, conservadores que deambularon por las extremas derechas y acabaron en el refugio de los valores socialistas, hoy tachados de románticos idealistas. Hay pocos, pero los hay.

Finalmente, hay un tercer caso de político cuántico: la mutación en adalid salvador de España y de los españoles, figura hasta ahora sólo vista en los anuncios de limpieza. Este político cuántico es una especie de Crispín –el compañero de aventuras del Capitán Trueno– que intenta, nada menos, entrar en un cesto repleto de manzanas podridas con la finalidad de sanarlas y sin contagiarse. En realidad más parece que es héroe de su propio ombligo, pues aquí la cuántica no le favorece: mientras que él acaba de llegar hace apenas tres años, la maceración de las élites del cesto podrido son, ni más ni menos, que los puntos suspensivos de un golpe militar que nos trajo una Guerra Civil, aunque eso sí, hoy son elegidos democráticamente.

Es obvio que Crispín llega con la cabeza ya torcida, vendiendo necesidades en nombre de todos los españoles e ignorando, a su vez, a más de trece millones de votantes que dicen estar hartos del cesto que ha elegido. Uno se pregunta si es ético recibir cada una de las ofensas de estas *rara avis*. ¿Acaso se puede robar y atropellar a un anciano voluntariamente y después tratar de ayudarle a levantase?

Hagamos un ejercicio de reflexión: cerremos por un momento los ojos e imaginemos el mundo que nos rodea con tan solo un tercio de las bondades de sus promesas electorales. Ahora volvamos al mundo real: tras casi cuarenta años de promesas, cada día veo más rejas en una jaula que no parece tener puerta de salida.

Por último están los otros políticos: los de abajo, los que siempre miran hacia arriba. Son los ciudadanos que sustentan, con las miserias que les dejan, tanta hipocresía y tanta vileza; los que tan solo piden, lo que ya para muchos es una entelequia, que se respete su dignidad.

El adjetivo 'socialista'

Publicado por infoLibre 18/07/2016

En los últimos tiempos, parecemos asistir a un continuo movimiento de tierra que hace perder equilibrios a los partidos políticos que han dejado atrás, la arrogancia de la suficiencia electoral por motivo de sus políticas. Si bien, el Partido Popular, empecinado con el maltrato social, intenta una y otra vez, como autoritario conservador que es, además de corrupto, arañar espacios en lugares ajenos donde reside la cordura y conducta de justicia social para volver a cometer nuevas tropelías, es al Partido Socialista Obrero Español, hoy metido en un lodazal donde el adjetivo socialista, asentado en valores de libertad, fraternidad e igualdad, es vilmente manoseado y ultrajado por intereses más afines a los mercados propios del capitalismo, es, como digo, a quien quiero dirigirme como socialista convencido y, en particular, a alguno de sus viejos militantes, a los que quisiera poner tildes que parecen haber olvidado.

Por ello, a esos egocéntricos socialistas que se han convertido en privilegiados nobles gracias al grito de justicia social de millones de votos vilmente traicionados; a esos que se han convertido en mesiánicos héroes utilizando las esperanzas de su pueblo, a esos que vuelven, como alimañas, a salir a la palestra para pedirnos alianzas con partidos antagónicos a la democracia, herederos de políticas dictatoriales y con estructuras corruptas desde la base como se demuestra a diario; a esa gente que hace llamadas de auxilio para oponerse a que se vote a partidos que recogen la indignación de sus políticas, a los decepcionados, a los humillados, ahora desplazados, poco menos, que en un gueto marginal de esperanza. A esos me refiero, a los *felipes*, a los *guerras*, a los *leguinas*, a los *serras*, a los *corcueras* y a muchos etcéteras que deambulan por esta sociedad que creen haber inventado con manifiestos tramposos de libertadores bananeros; a estos salvadores de la patria que se atreven descaradamente a mostrarnos, cada vez que asoman sus fauces, pancartas de: "Yo he traído la libertad" o "la enseñanza universal que tenemos es gracias a nosotros" o "el divorcio es por nosotros" o el mismísimo "aborto lo aprobamos nosotros" y así un sin fin de elocuentes discursos que parecen justificar sus nuevos trajes y que en modo alguno legitima su bastardo mensaje a un pueblo desplazado, que sigue esperando equidad y justicia social. A esos que lo que realmente han conseguido para su pueblo, tras varios gobiernos, es tan solo crear otra marca España con la que nos insultan diariamente.

A esos vendedores de sabidurías mezquinas, ya tan narcisistas, les sugiero desde la indignación, que observen sus ombligos, si es que creen que aún los tienen, y midan la equidistancia de igualdad social que tienen respecto del pueblo que les votó hace ya mucho tiempo y que se vistan de honradez, al menos por una vez en sus vidas y devuelvan el adjetivo de "socialista" a quien verdaderamente le corresponde que no es otro que al pueblo indignado por el abuso de sus políticas antisociales. Ustedes ni son socialistas, ni son obreros, ni siquiera españoles, y no lo son, porque ya españolean como los otros. A esos, a ustedes que bastardamente ensucian a diario la dignidad de llamarse "socialistas" les deseo que sigan teniendo un buen viaje al paraíso de la opulencia bien acompañados del adjetivo de "indeseables". Y a esos otros que aún quedan en el atrio de la casa socialista les hago participes de un deseo manifiesto de mucha gente, que no es otro, que el de abrir ventanas que oreen vilezas ya anquilosadas para un rápido retorno a la casa de todos los socialistas desplazados.

Defender la Constitución española

Publicado por infoLibre 06/07/2016

Igual que ayer, tras una elecciones, el partido mayoritario, el partido con mayores corruptelas sentenciadas en España ha vuelto a hacer de su capa un sayo. Si ayer, el señor Rajoy justificaba el rechazo a su programa electoral por la pésima gestión de su antecesor Zapatero, trayendo la reforma laboral y la subida de impuestos, hoy, apenas unos días tras las elecciones, ha vuelto a saquear, impunemente, la hucha de las pensiones, esto es, otros 8.700 millones del fondo de reserva de las pensiones contributivas.

Y como las vergüenzas no vienen solas hoy, amanecemos con la noticia de que una gestora se hará cargo del Partido Popular en Palma por vínculos con una red corrupta que, parece ser, no es la del propio partido con todo lo que ha llovido sobre él. "Acabar con todo", esa y no otra parece ser la consigna del Partido Popular. Salarios paupérrimos, contratos basura, *ley mordaza*, la reforma del artículo 135, aniquilar el estado del bienestar, o ahora, desmantelar el Fondo de Reserva de las Pensiones es lo que toca, seguramente justificándolo con un nuevo adjetivo, un nuevo Zapatero de turno.

Junto a las incesantes esquelas del deterioro democrático que diariamente asoman en los medios de comunicación con corruptelas del partido ganador de las últimas tres elecciones y que, aún, tiene cerca de ocho millones de votos apoyando sus desmanes con fariseísmos impropios de sociedades avanzadas, le hacen a uno pensar en cómo proteger a una democracia, ya de pandereta, que éstos nuevos demócratas que arrasan abocándonos a un futuro desmoralizador. Cabe preguntarse si es legítimo e incluso democrático aceptar las urnas aún sabiendo que quien tiene que gobernar se dedica a la desmembrar la propia Constitución, aboliendo derechos constitucionales primarios de equidad y de igualdad.

La historia justifica esta aparente injusticia con casos como el de Hitler en Alemania, utilizando las vías democráticas para conseguir dictaduras frente a sus ciudadanos. Hoy, en España, ya nadie piensa que todos somos iguales ante la ley, que tenemos los mismos derechos y privilegios, ni siquiera lo piensan los que han votado al Partido Popular, porque a ellos, esto de la democracia, véase sus votos, siempre les ha importado un bledo. Ya se ha dicho muchas veces que los que jalean a este partido jalean igualmente y en la misma dirección el empobrecimiento democrático frente a la indignación de nobles ciudadanos. Acudo a este adjetivo "nobles" porque hasta ellos mismos, los que han votado a un partido corrupto, saben, por mucho que lo escondan que es un adjetivo donde se puede vivir.

Hoy la tan pobre, y ya muy vieja, Constitución no deja de ser un mero enunciado más de un grafiti; parece aparcada frente a un brasero ajena a todo lo que pasa, como esas mujeres, ya ancianas, que parecen molestar en casa después de haberte dado la vida. ¿Cómo defenderla pues de estos desmanes, nos preguntamos los, aún, constitucionalistas? ¿Cómo se puede defender, semejante señora con loas a la corrupción y al saqueo, aunque sea en forma de voto? ¿Acaso es permisible que un país se pueda permitir por mayoría vivir corruptamente? Es la propia Constitución quien debe defenderse de estos abusos, vistiéndola con librea que repela ataques que mine la moral de su propio pueblo. ¿Cómo? Deben ser los políticos quien busquen recursos para ello y no para ellos, como lo han estado haciendo. Si la grandeza de la Constitución está por encima de los partidos, ¿por qué no blindarla frente a éstos?

Si la Constitución es la casa común de todos y nos protege a todos por igual, tanto a los unos como a los otros, a excepción de la Casa Real, ¿por qué no la protegemos frente a mayorías que buscan nocivas artimañas para deslegitimarla convirtiéndola en adúltera? Por todo lo dicho lo único que parece claro es que los ciudadanos y los partidos caminan por rumbos diferentes. Unos buscando derechos y libertades que los iguale; los otros beneficios que los distinga. Da igual si son nuevos o viejos, lo hemos visto en estas dos últimas elecciones. Los viejos partidos a lo suyo, incluso, buscándose como dos enamorados; los nuevos, innovando postureo, los de Albert mostrando el mismo ADN con tintes más joviales para '*ucedizar*' el PP, el de Pablo Iglesias convertido en un fauno absolutamente perdido en su laberinto, tan perdido que tan solo le hizo falta un día para tirar todo lo conseguido por tierra, tras la gran cosecha de votos de diciembre con su apuesta por el referéndum catalán, frente a la indignación social que fue lo que ocurrió realmente durante el 15M. Tergiversar un hecho tan relevante en la historia de España ya es una mezquindad.

Señor iglesias, en ninguna plaza se habló de dicho referéndum como prioridad, había indignación social por los desmanes de los políticos con sus políticas, como así lo manifestasteis en vuestra propia campaña electoral. ¿A qué viene dar prioridad a un hecho secundario como es el referéndum frente a la indignación? ¿Qué es de la emergencia social a la que tanto aludisteis? ¿Quizás refrendando vuestro mesianismo con la puesta en escena de *El adefesio* de Alberti, queriendo suplantar al Che Guevara bajando del asalto al cielo y ofreciéndose poco menos que una ristra de ministerios y cargos al mejor estilo *far west* de John Wayne? Ristra que muchos de sus votantes, entre los que me encuentro, la han convertido en ajos, para luchar contra el mal fario de su joven mesías, hoy ya abocado a ceder su sitio en el cielo. Permítanme ya para terminar esta ristra de palabras, alentar a la defensa de la democracia con una Constitución que se proteja tanto de las veleidades de los partidos políticos, como de los mecenas salvadores de patrias. Ya lo decía Roosevelt: "Una democracia debe progresar o pronto dejará de ser o grande o democracia", aunque solo sea por ser ella. La Constitución española es hasta el momento, aunque parezca papel mojado, la única que nos protege, nos iguala y nos respeta al común de los ciudadanos de este país llamado España.

Satisfecho

Publicado en página del autor 28/05/2014

Vaya, vaya... después de observar lo que ha pasado este 25 de mayo con la votaciones europeas que más parecen "caseras", pues creo que se ha votado nuestra política y a nuestros políticos, hoy me siento un poco menos harto que estos tiempos pasados. Sí, yo diría satisfecho. Satisfecho por varios motivos. En primer lugar por divisar que se puede parar los desmanes de los sinvergüenzas y corruptos que nos han gobernado y nos gobiernan. Hoy 25 de mayo, al menos diecisiete escaños menos en Europa de éstos partidos, se quedan sin los privilegios que se han dado así mismo y sin escuchar las protestas de sus ciudadanos. Los que los sustituyen al menos y por el momento no han demostrado las destrezas del engaño para con su buena vida. Ya ganamos en algo. Ya lo decía en mi anterior ¡Sigo estando harto! Publicado el 26 de Julio de 2013.También ganamos en democracia visto el nerviosismo que les ha causado el movimiento "Podemos", solamente hay que ver los insultos y descalificaciones que les profesan a esta nueva formación política la batería de medios de comunicación afines al poder. Esto nos demuestra que una gran masa adormecida ante tanta corrupción ha despertado. ¡Bienvenidos de nuevo a la democracia! Seguro que esto les hará ser menos descarados, más cautos y lo digo pensando no por lo que hagan en el poder sino porque estarán en sus casas y... hacerlo en sus bolsillos lo que han hecho con lo de los demás... Como seguro que obligará a partidos teóricamente democráticos, a plantearse y redefinir qué es y para qué sirve la democracia. Sí, me siento muy satisfecho.

¿Han dejado de chillar esos corderos, Clarice?

Publicado en página del autor 21/03/2014

Llámenlo como ustedes quieran, postilla, posdata o simplemente una anotación más a mis "harturas" ya publicadas. Ya sé que en mi última intervención me propuse acabar con mis exabruptos, pero siempre hay un catarro que curar, o dicho de otra manera, mientras existan las enfermedades siempre habrá medicamentos que tomar. En estos días un nuevo esfuerzo de miles de ciudadanos de todos los puntos de España, indignados con lo que está sucediendo vuelven a mostrar su rabia contra la Jauría de lobos hambrientos que se postulan indefinidamente en las instituciones públicas al amparo de partidos corruptos que con un cinismo desmedido muestran cada día sus tropelías convirtiendo nuestra añorada democracia en una feudal dictadura. Con desprecio, también cada día oigo más los silencios de un pueblo abatido por el yugo de la corrupción política, por la voracidad de la banca, por el autismo europeo, ...mundial, y por la mordaza de periodistas asalariados que en ningún modo ejercen la idiosincrasia de la enseñanza recibida en sus facultades, ya a veces, me pregunto, si éstas son necesarias, pues más parecen fabricas de "matriuskas" que de libres pensadores y lo digo porque siempre se pregonan así mismo, como "garantes de la libertad". Alguien diría: los polos opuestos se atraen. No, en política, sobre todo, los sinvergüenzas se atraen, al menos eso es la demostración palpable que durante los años de "libertad" nos mostraron nuestros políticos. Sí, por momentos me parece escuchar "¿...han dejado de chillar esos corderos, Clarice?. En breve nuevas elecciones, donde aparecerán los encantadores de serpientes, los mismos que hace treinta y muchos años, los mismos que han aniquilado las esperanzas de todo un pueblo por sus desmanes, pidiéndoles otro esfuerzo, su voto, para continuar insaciables, llenando sus bolsillos cuales personajillos de novela como Félix Grandet, el avaro tonelero de Balzac o el mismísimo Harpagón de "El Avaro" de Moliere, todos convirtiendo en protagonista al "miedo", unos por utilizarlo, otros por "guardar la viña". Sí, parece que asistimos al "Gran teatro del mundo" pero no solo al de nuestro Calderón de la Barca, por cierto, no les vendría mal leerla a estos caballeros que a diario distorsionan voluntariamente la realidad, seguro que se identificarían inmediatamente con sus personajes, me refiero a la contemplación de un pueblo que es mero espectador de su propia agonía, recordándome, no sé por qué, el capítulo de "El heroísmo de la obediencia pasiva" que escribió Víctor Hugo en su obra "Los miserables" en 1862. Eran otros tiempos, sí, eran otros tiempos... Sí, sigamos contemplando la belleza del espectáculo, con palomitas en la mano, esperando que confluyan el fin de la película, tú película, con el fin de tu dignidad, al fin y al cabo, ese es el precio de las banalidades, quizás para entonces sea tarde, siendo otros quienes puedan algún día escuchar el silencio de los corderos... Yo, de momento aprovecharé un "intermedio" para ir este sábado a paliar la indignación de miles de personas que ya han perdido sus hogares, sus trabajos, sus derechos, sus libertades... este y no otro, es por el momento mi medicamento.

¡Harto de estar harto!

Publicado en página del autor 09/12/2013

En este, mi tercer exabrupto y ya terminando el año, quiero aprovechar para felicitar la navidad a cuantos en algún momento leyeron mis palabras e igualmente para desearles un venidero año nuevo con una imagen, que nos deja este final de año y que no es otra que la de Nelson Mandela. Una imagen de esperanza. Pero también una imagen de nostalgia, una imagen de rabia, y una imagen de humildad. De nostalgia por haber conocido a todo un hombre comprometido con la desigualdad social, que nos mostró una vez más, el camino a seguir desde la humildad y el perdón con la crueldad de algunos hombres que se empecinan por ser cada día más poderosos a costa de los esfuerzos de los más débiles. Pero también una imagen de rabia, ahora llegarán "los hombres de gris" como los llamaba Michael Ende, en la novela *Momo,* y los veremos en primera fila, cuales cuervos, al olor de la muerte, en busca de su tajada y donde pocos, o muy pocos dedicarán un minuto a reflexionar sobre la vida del difunto, sobre el porqué de sus veintiocho años en prisión, porque pocos de cuantos estén ahí, velándole, han sabido entender aquella valiosa "Carta de libertad" que se aprobó en el Congreso Nacional Africano en mil novecientos cincuenta y cinco y que hablaba de peticiones tan humanas como las que actualmente estamos pidiendo. No las voy a nombrar. Son las más básicas para hacer de un hombre, una persona, también las más elementales para consolidar una democracia. Sí, muchos de ellos estarán en primera fila glorificando su gesta e ignorando sus palabras. Sí, estarán en la primera fila mostrándonos su cinismo, cómo llaman democracia a la *chequedemocracia*, permitiendo el uso de paraísos fiscales donde guardan los esfuerzos de sus pueblos, donde dan cobijo a grandes tesoros usurpados a los ciudadanos, cuales piratas, lo que ya en sí mismo y ante todo el mundo, por el mero hecho de permitirlo y con el mayor de los descaros, les hace auto inculparse como delincuentes, dictando a su vez medidas arbitrarias para aflorar miserias necesarias para supervivencia a los más desfavorecidos e igualmente dictando para ellos medidas de blanqueo, trayendo hasta nuestros días el diezmo medieval, un diezmo político y civil que enriquece a la "nobleza" con el esfuerzo de los más débiles. Sí, estarán en primera fila y con honores, ávidos por que las cámaras les encuentren para divulgar sus proclamas que traerán ya escritas por sus cientos de asesores para cautivar al pueblo, con el único objetivo de buscar en ellos votos que prolonguen su boato, sus "cenas santas" que endiosan sus egos y... sus miserias, cuales buitres acechando el manjar del cadáver ya mencionado y regresando a sus países glorificados de humanidad para seguir subyugando a sus pueblos a las directrices de los delincuentes de guante blanco, esos que los amparan, dejando la pobreza que siga siendo contrarrestada por los anónimos ciudadanos de todo el mundo en organizaciones no gubernamentales en lucha contra el autismo institucional que ellos mismos han cimentado, asumiendo la mezquindad de sus políticas y por ello, de sus oficios. Pero también, un día como hoy, la imagen de "Madiba", como le gustaba que le llamaran, nos profesa humildad y nos refresca nuestro ego, al menos el mío, enseñándome que también el camino del exabrupto no es el más adecuado por carecer de paciencia, por ser en sí mismo, intolerante... él lo supo hacer en la sombra, durante veintiocho años, yo no he aprendido en cincuenta. Quizás por ello, o mejor dicho por él, me propongo acabar con mis exabruptos de estar harto.

¡Sigo estando harto!

Publicado en página del autor 26/07/2013

¡Sigo estando harto!. Muy harto y muy cabreado ante todo lo que sigue sucediendo en nuestro país, muy cabreado y enojado con la clase política en particular y con el deterioro del Estado de Derecho en general. También con la ciudadanía. Muchas veces me he preguntado, ¿dónde está nuestro espíritu crítico y revolucionario de otros tiempos?, ¿hasta cuándo y cuánto estamos dispuestos a aguantar?. Nos quitan los derechos ganados en treinta y cinco años, en una abrir y cerrar de ojos, "ellos" los consolidan y aumentan eternizándolos; las listas del paro rompen diariamente las estadísticas, aumentando constantemente, "ellos" se perpetúan en sus cargos; nuestros hijos, tienen que emigrar por falta de trabajo, "ellos" viven en paraísos fiscales continuados; los salarios bajan, "ellos se los suben"; privatizan todo lo público, "ellos" engrandecen sus patrimonios personales; sube la

luz, el agua, el gas para pagar "pequeñas" prebendas a "sus" ex dirigentes parlamentarios, bien
acomodados en "sus" ex empresas públicas,
blindándose sueldos cual capos de la banca y por
ende de la política, e incluso otorgándose asimismo indultos, sin pudor alguno, exhibiendo su im-
punidad frente al escepticismo del pueblo. Ya hoy
en día nadie en el mundo se cree que en España
exista la separación e independencia de poderes,
como ya nadie cree en "ellos", en estos catedráticos
de todo y maestrillos de nada. ¿Qué necesitamos
para reaccionar?. Sinceramente no lo sé, pero me
debo a mi conciencia y ella me pide que reaccione
y reacciono creyendo que ha llegado el momento
de empezar de nuevo. Y "nuevo" quiere decir ni un
solo apoyo más a ningún partido que esté repre-
sentado actualmente en el Parlamento. Así, como
suena. ¿Por qué?. Sin duda porque no es cierto que
vivamos es un Estado de Derecho, porque no es
cierto que todos seamos iguales ante la ley, no voy
a enumerar casos de unos y otros, ustedes ya lo

saben, diariamente nos llegan noticias de ello, principalmente porque una "Constitución" debe garantizar los derechos de sus ciudadanos y éstos impunemente han sido saqueados principalmente por los dos grandes partidos, permítanme no hacerles publicidad, me deprime el solo hecho de mencionarlos, ellos han gobernado el Estado Español durante el mayor tiempo democrático, a capricho, arrasándolo y haciendo culpable a la ciudadanía de su patética gestión, de sus muchas deudas contraídas que han llenado sus bolsillos, extremando la estrechez de los del ciudadano haciéndonos culpables de su vileza, pero también por el resto de las fuerzas representadas en el parlamento (lo pongo con minúscula voluntariamente porque siento vergüenza de todos ellos) sí, porque siendo así y viendo como se ningunea lo conseguido en tantos años, éstos minoritarios partidos y por supuesto que todos legitimados con el voto, deberían voluntariamente no participar en esta a debacle de "surrealista democracia", sumándose así, a la indignación del país, dejando en precario, y ante los ojos del mundo a un gobierno que gobierna, cual dictador, vía decreto, haciendo de su "capa un sayo" e ignorando el espíritu democrático del voto. Insisto, "espíritu democrático del voto", sin duda, muchos de cuantos ocupan esos grandes partidos ignoran qué significa. En un Estado moderno, las democracias no permiten, aun teniendo esas mayorías, que puedan ser capaces de autodestruirse, eso ya paso en Alemania con Hitler, deben estar blindadas a esos posibles ataques de mediocres e ineptos ególatras, que como pasa en este país en lugar de blindar derechos de la ciudadanía, blindan sueldos de sinvergüenzas.

Por ello, creo que debemos, en primer lugar y desde la base, empezar en los pequeños municipios, evitando el voto a quién se postula en nombre de esos partidos, e invitándoles a que formen parte de un nuevo proyecto común, e incluso que lo lideren si fuese necesario, pero unidos. Con ello conseguiremos un buen puñado de buenos resultados y como no, de razones. Uno y una, si no consiguen votos los actuales partidos, ningún holgazán de "capital" seguirá estando en el Parlamento, Senado, Bruselas, Diputaciones, etc. etc., como hasta el momento con privilegios de "Césares" aun habiendo siendo culpable del actual estado en el que nos encontramos. En segundo lugar, conseguiríamos un propósito prioritario, caminar todos en el mismo barco, remando en la misma dirección con decisiones que nos atañen por vecindad, ¿no utilizamos las misma aceras y respiramos el mismo aire, como decía en mi anterior exabrupto? Cambiaríamos el parlamento de los partidos por el Parlamento de los pueblos. Otra mejora, importante sin duda, sería la soberanía en las decisiones, sin ataduras a la codicia de los bancos y cajas que convierten a los partidos en meros adláteres por hipotecas contraídas, así evitaríamos ser víctimas de su propia usura; ¿Por qué seguir con ellos?, creemos uno, sin más, sin ligaduras que le impida tomar decisiones. Les aseguro que podría enumerar muchísimas mejoras más, ustedes también, pero no lo voy a hacer, tan solo les diré que la aventura, además de dar respuesta a mi estado crítico y por lo tanto, caprichosa, creo, es también, muy positiva y hasta fácil, muy fácil, porque ¿no creen ustedes que por mal que se hiciera, y sinceramente no lo creo y por mucho que nos costase, el nuevo grupo, partido, llámenle ustedes como quieran, no lo iba a hacer mejor, mucho mejor, que los actuales? Ellos ya han demostrado su incompetencia, llevan treinta y cinco años apostados en los gobiernos: Local, Autonómico y Central, dilapidando el dinero de los ciudadanos, saqueando cuanto tiene el patrimonio público, han dejado las administraciones como un solar, mientras ellos se han llenado privadamente de solares; se han cargado una Constitución de todos para hacerla de "ellos", a su medida, y si alguna duda queda, miren a sus principales cabecillas, ¿Acaso no estaban en los primeros años de democracia? ¿De qué nos van a salvar ahora?

Quiero permitirme unas palabras a esas personas, más cercanas, siempre vecinos, algunas amigas, que actualmente están enarbolando los logotipos, estandartes o signos orgullosos de esas formaciones políticas, que nos han llevado a la actual crisis y que sin duda son ajenas a decisiones de sus superiores orgánicamente y que han deteriorado la vida de todos los españoles, incluso de sus familiares. A ellos en particular, no alcanzo a ver, qué, o cuál es el entusiasmo que les hace aún, empuñar dichos signos ante la catástrofe que han creado sus endiosados líderes, ¿qué clase de usura, hace que un ciudadano que humillado con restricciones propias de una posguerra, aún y sin vergüenza, pida el voto para estos líderes que han mostrado por activa y por pasiva su mezquindad haciéndose pasar por demócratas?; ¿qué diabólicos intereses suscita a ir contra tus vecinos, amigos y familiares, sometiéndoles diariamente a la dictadura de las decisiones de vuestros líderes qué jamás han mostrado un ápice de gratitud para con tu pueblo?; ¿realmente os creéis que nos sentimos mejor al amparo de la codicia de vuestros caudillos? Ya han demostrado su ineptitud. ¿por qué seguir validándolos? Uníos a la indignación del pueblo y permitirnos poner freno a sus insaciables ambiciones.

Y por último sólo decirles que no pretendo encabezar ningún partido, ni si quiera busco apoyo alguno, ni nada que se le parezca, si acaso, estimular mi conciencia.

¡Estoy Harto!

Publicado en página del autor 01/02/2013

Estoy harto, muy harto de cuanto está pasando con cada uno de nosotros, también de nosotros mismos. De cómo la codicia de unos pocos es capaz de arruinar a un país. De cómo la miseria de unos son utilizadas para engordar las de otros. De cómo un país puede ser saqueado literalmente y no ocurra nada. Estoy harto de llamar democracia a lo que es la dictadura de unos "malparidos" secuaces. De cómo unos pocos indecentes someten a un pueblo quitándoles derechos para convertirlos en propios privilegios. Estoy harto de indecentes mecenas que esclavizan a un pueblo para llenar sus estómagos.

Hartos de cuantos hablamos y no reaccionamos, de mi mismo. Sí estoy harto, muy harto de comprar miserias a precios demasiado elevados. De ver cada día a delincuentes en los medios de comunicación como maestros de la equidad y la justicia. Estoy harto de nosotros mismos, de ver como protegemos a los sinvergüenzas con nuestros votos. Sí, estoy harto y es por ello que apoyo a movimientos que denuncien el abuso de los valores democráticos de quienes se creen propietarios del voto del ciudadano para colmar intereses privados. Detesto esta nueva casta de políticos, banqueros y periodistas que viven solo para sus estómagos, utilizando el voto como mera moneda de cambio y como pago de hipotecas contraídas entre sí. Rechazo a quienes someten a un pueblo a pagar crisis que solo los poderosos pueden generar; y desprecio a quienes han menospreciado tantos años la lucha obrera por conseguir una justa convivencia entre todos, para hacer de ella, un tapete de juego donde repartirse a capricho prebendas ajenas. Y por último me solidarizo con la única vaca que se pasea por todo el mundo soportando más de dieciocho gobiernos chupando de su teta, Si estoy harto.

Mi apoyo

Publicado en página del autor octubre de 2011

Apoyo movimientos que denuncien el abuso de los valores democráticos de quienes se creen propietarios del voto del ciudadano para colmar intereses privados. Detesto esta nueva casta de políticos, banqueros y periodistas que viven solo para sus estómagos, utilizando el voto como mera moneda de cambio y como pago de hipotecas contraídas entre sí. Rechazo a quienes someten a un pueblo a pagar crisis que solo los poderosos pueden generar; y desprecio a quienes han menospreciado tantos años de lucha obrera por conseguir una justa convivencia entre todos, para hacer de ella, un tapete de juego donde repartirse a capricho prebendas ajenas. Y por último me solidarizo con la única "vaca" que se pasea por todo el mundo soportando más de 18 gobiernos, chupando de su teta. Y ahora sí termino, diciendo que me indigna que ni un solo político haya salido a la palestra defen-

diéndose de los insultos de corrupción que movimientos como el 15-m han denunciado por todo el
mundo. Por todo ello yo también apoyo al 15-m
¡por sentirme indignado!